Colin E. Gunton is Professor of Christian Doctrine at King's College, University of London.

THE DOCTRINE OF CREATION

THE DOCTRINE OF CREATION

ESSAYS IN DOGMATICS, HISTORY AND PHILOSOPHY

Edited by
Colin E. Gunton
for the
Research Institute in Systematic Theology
King's College, London

T&T CLARK
EDINBURGH

T&T CLARK LTD
59 GEORGE STREET
EDINBURGH EH2 2LQ
SCOTLAND

First published 1997

ISBN 0 567 08588 0

British Library Cataloguing-in-Publication Data
A catalogue record for this book is available from the British Library

Typeset by Waverley Typesetters, Galashiels
Printed and bound in Great Britain by Bookcraft Ltd, Avon

Contents

Introduction
Colin E. Gunton

I   Time for Reconsideration?

It is not too much of an exaggeration to say that in the modern world the doctrine of creation has in many places given way to discussions of the relation between science and religion. This is partly the result of the laicisation of the doctrine in the early modern age,[1] partly of an even earlier tendency to restrict or prepare for its discussion in what is effectively natural theology. There have been, and increasingly are, exceptions: notably Barth's rich dogmatic exposition, marred though it is – as he himself acknowledged – by its almost complete lack of reference to science; and, more recently, the work of Moltmann, discussed in chapter 5 below, and Pannenberg's fine trinitarian construction of the doctrine, which does take account of science.[2] In general, however, properly dogmatic treatments are few and far between, so that this volume is an attempt to begin to fill at least some of the gaps. The matter of science, though not completely absent, is left on one side, though a companion volume is in preparation which will to some extent compensate. The centre of this book, however, is to be found in a range of attempts to state the main features of the Christian understanding of creation, in both historical and systematic relations.

In that they are concerned in large measure with divine action in and towards the world of time and space, the puzzles of the doctrine of creation are parallel to those of christology, yet different in important respects. One difference is that whereas the doctrine of the incarnation speaks of the inter-action of eternity and time in history, at a time that can be approximately located, the same can by no means be said of the doctrine of creation. It is indeed concerned with the interaction of the eternal God and the world he has made. But

[1] Amos Funkenstein, *Theology and the Scientific Imagination from the Middle Ages to the Seventeenth Century* (Princeton: Princeton University Press, 1986).
[2] Wolfhart Pannenberg, *Systematic Theology*, vol. 2, translated by Geoffrey W. Bromiley (Edinburgh: T. & T. Clark, 1994).

1

whereas christology concerns God's involvement in a world 'already' made, creation is to do with the constituting of that world 'in the beginning'.[3] In those latter words, taken as they are from one translation of the first verse of the book of Genesis, is to be found the heart of the problem.[4] The reason is that one clue to the nature of a doctrine of creation is the way in which it conceives the relation between eternity and time. If it is to be meaningfully described as a doctrine of creation, however minimal may be the conception, something must be articulated about the relation between that which precedes the created world, whether ontologically or in terms of time also, and that which is in whatever sense caused by it. It might be said, without much exaggeration, that in recent centuries most theologians, with some notable exceptions, have handed over the making of such an account to science, or what is thought to be science. The result is that when science apparently requires a deterministic or mechanistic view of the relation between the eternal and the temporal, Christian theology at least is hard pressed to maintain its traditional voice which speaks of the free creation of the world by a personal God. To be sure, the effect can be exaggerated, and has been, as in John Dillenberger's characterisation of nineteenth-century disarray: 'the late nineteenth and early twentieth centuries may have been one of the rare periods in history in which theology was virtually impossible, when the crisis of language and imagination excluded the essential depth of both God and man'.[5] It must be remembered that the nineteenth century was also that of Michael Faraday and James Clerk Maxwell, makers of twentieth-century physics and men who engaged in science because they believed in the Christian doctrine of creation, not because they found it an irrelevance or hindrance.

Today, things are much changed, although there is a degree to which the leading proponents of versions of the doctrine of creation, whether in generally Christian or Eastern religious form, are still the scientists. Doctrines of creation in the broad sense of accounts of the universe which refer its being in some way or other to persons or forces transcendent of that universe in however tenuous a sense, abound: almost a case of how many

---

[3] The point of the quotation marks will become evident from the contents of the essays.

[4] 'In the beginning' may not be the most accurate translation, but that is not relevant to the point being made here, which is that historically, discussion has been dominated by debates about the meaning of this particular form of words.

[5] John Dillenberger, *Protestant Thought and Natural Science* (London: Collins, 1961), p. 253.

cosmologists, so many theologies of creation. Even Hawking's largely anti-theological account of the origin of the universe occasionally uses the term 'God' in its speculations.[6] And leading scientists who are Christian believers also often shape their accounts of creation as a divine act by abstracting from features of the observed and theorised universe that they believe to be open to a theological account.[7]

But so important is this matter that it cannot be left to the scientists, for if creation is a theological question, then it is necessary that theologians should offer their relatively independent account of what it is that they believe the doctrine to teach. There was a tradition of creation theology before Newton – indeed, his mechanistic world-view was anticipated in the work of mediaeval thinkers centuries before[8] – and in the twentieth century there have been, as we have already noted, at least three original trinitarian dogmatics of creation, whether or not they are considered to engage adequately with the characteristic challenges of our scientifically dominated culture. It was with considerations such as this in mind that the Research Institute in Systematic Theology called a conference specifically to discuss central aspects of the dogmatics of creation, widely interpreted to mean aspects of creation on which Christian theology might be conceived to have a bearing.

Four aspects came under review. The first is dogmatics proper: simply attempting to state what it means for Christian theology to affirm that God is the creator of the universe. Much time is spent in the papers in discussion of the credal form of the doctrine – 'I believe in God the Father almighty, maker of heaven and earth' – and the classical discussions of that in St. Augustine, the father of all Western theology, in particular. Readers of this volume will find much criticism of Augustine, but also some defence, for it is of the essence of this protean thinker that he reviews a range of positions, not all of them consistent with one another, so that the dogmatic and philosophical doctrines which he rejects often form the basis of different later developments. Not surprisingly, it is his many-sided reflections on the nature of time and its relation to eternity that feature in a number of the papers.

---

[6] Stephen Hawking, *A Brief History of Time. From the Big Bang to Black Holes* (London: Bantam Press, 1988).

[7] Arthur Peacocke, *Creation and the World of Science* (Oxford: Clarendon Press, 1979), is perhaps the finest extended account of such a possibility.

[8] The evidence for this can be found in Toby E. Huff, *The Rise of Early Modern Science. Islam, China and the West* (Cambridge: Cambridge University Press, 1993), e.g. p. 41.

The second aspect is the historical. For many reasons, the
thesis associated with Harnack that the Christian gospel came
to be contaminated with foreign elements which changed it
into something else is more defensible in this case than in the
case of christology and the doctrine of the Trinity. In the latter
two cases it is arguable that things were said there – in the
homoousion and the concept of the *koinonia* and *perichoresis* of
the persons of the Trinity – that were simply impossible in
terms of the Greek philosophy which they effectively undermined. In the case of creation, however, the intellectual revolution which was promised never took place – or rather did not
take place until the Reformation, if even then – for the very
reason that it is in respect of the theology of creation that the
fusion of philosophy and theology was most disabling but often
least apparent.

At the centre of this many-sided matter is the question of
christology. Not only is creation understood by many New
Testament writers to be 'through Christ', but in patristic
writers like Irenaeus and Athanasius christology was the key
to the doctrine of creation. It was christology which enabled
the emergence of the doctrine of creation, and particularly
creation out of nothing, which effectively overturned all the
assumptions of Greek and other philosophy that the universe,
or some universe, was eternal. It was christology which enabled
theology to conceive of a relation of God to the world, of eternity
to time, in which the two are *both* contingently *and* internally,
rather than necessarily or externally related. (If this had been
maintained, deism and pantheism would never have been as
plausible as they have both been at different times.) Further,
it is christology which enables theology to hold together
creation and redemption. If creation is not thought of christologically in that connection, the danger is always present of
either a narrowly anthropocentric conception of redemption
that relativises the importance of the created order or a semi-
gnostic conception of human life which finds it difficult to relate
soul to body and to maintain the importance of the latter – or,
more likely, of both. As Brian Horne shows in his paper, this
had serious implications for the Western understanding of art,
but historically the effect has been more serious across a whole
range of doctrine and forms of life.

The third aspect is the philosophical and it brings to the
fore puzzles which have been, certainly since the definitive
work of Augustine of Hippo, inextricable from any theological
treatment of the topic. Here we see the ambivalence of the
historical development of the doctrine, for this great thinker at
once broke the chains of Hellenistic determinism *and* tied it to

other features of Greek thought which militate against a theological realisation of the full reality of the material world. For Augustine, the world is sometimes affirmed as good – because it is the product of the will of God – sometimes denigrated as 'next to nothing'[9] because he still thinks in terms of a Neoplatonist hierarchy of being. The result is that sometimes he affirms that the world is created with time and space, but at others appears to take away with the left hand what is given with the right, asserting that the whole process of creation is instantaneous. Both of these ambivalences require careful philosophical discussion if the wholeness of the doctrine is to be maintained.

The fourth aspect is what can generally be referred to as the moral, not in a restricted sense, but as concerned with forms of human action in and towards the world. In papers on these aspects, the hope was to move beyond the largely ecological – though that can never be absent in a modern context, and does come under review in Professor Schwöbel's paper – to include other dimensions, and specifically the aesthetic, for art involves one of the many human ways of relating to the material world. The historical problem here is that there has been a tendency to concentrate on the largely notional aspects of the doctrine of creation. That is to say, so anxious have theologians been to demonstrate the credibility of the doctrine of creation by using the natural world to provide evidence of its truth, that the reverse relation has been neglected. What implications might a doctrine of creation have for human life in the world? Here, with his extended treatment of the ethics of creation, Barth provides a model who has been rarely imitated, but other recent treatments, with the exception of Oliver O'Donovan's seminal *Resurrection and Moral Order*, are thin on the ground indeed.[10]

II

While all four of the above aspects have been treated in the papers presented in this collection, they are not treated in that order, for two reasons. The first is that more than one of the topics have been treated in some of the chapters, and there is much overlap between them all. The second is that the order of presentation has been arranged both to establish priorities and

---

[9] Augustine, *Conf.* 12.7.
[10] Karl Barth, *Church Dogmatics* translation edited by G. W. Bromiley and T. F. Torrance (Edinburgh: T. & T. Clark, 1957–69), 3/4; Oliver O'Donovan, *Resurrection and Moral Order. An Outline for Evangelical Ethics* (Leicester: IVP, 1986).

also to enrich discussion as the book proceeds. In order to establish the priorities, the book is headed by one discussion whose centre is dogmatic, another whose orientation is chiefly philosophical. The dogmatic treatment is presented in the outline dogmatics of creation by Robert W. Jenson, 'Aspects of a Doctrine of Creation'. His opening point is that the doctrine of creation has its origin as an exegesis of scripture which took shape in the creed-making activities of the second- and third-century church as it was confronted with philosophical and mythological teaching that in various ways conflicted with the biblical faith. Professor Jenson articulates the main affirmations of the doctrine in a number of points. First, 'There *is* indeed other reality than God, and it is really other' (p. 18), and second this reality is dependent upon God's will. These polar points are then supplemented by two making a second polarity, that the doctrine is concerned to certify a present reality – that the world is dependent on God's will now – and yet at the same times declares that this reality has an absolute beginning. The two together guarantee what some theologies – for example those of Origen and Augustine – do not always adequately safeguard, that what we are concerned with in the doctrine of creation is not a timeless relation between God and the world but one which requires a notion of the relation between the eternal and time that better guarantees the reality and importance of the latter.

Jenson's two remaining points together take us to the heart of the point of the doctrine of creation. He argues that which has an absolute beginning has also a *termination*: that is to say, there is an end in view. This serves as an answer to the age-old and universal puzzle – Why is there anything rather than nothing? – to which the biblical doctrine gives a specific answer: 'the world is good in that it has been commanded to be good for the intent of the commander' (p. 22). And what is the content of that good? The answer can only be christological and ecclesiological: 'God is our end in that God the Son . . . is identified with a human community, the church, and in that the fulfilment of this identification is the purpose of our being' (p. 23).

What is the point of the introduction of these apparently tangential doctrines? They enable the author to bring together in the final section of the paper all of the adumbrated themes with a systematic account of the relation between God and the world which is implied by them. God creates in order to find a space in his triune life 'for others than the three whose mutual life he is' (p. 24). We now begin to realise why, according to this writer, it is unsatisfactory to posit a timeless relation between

God and the world, for 'time' is that place within the triune life which God creates for the reality that is other than himself. It is at this place that the author's reason for discomfort with Augustine's construal of the relation between time and eternity becomes clear in a sustained engagement with one feature of it. This centres on Augustine's interpretation of God as 'sheer Presence, that is, as sheer timeless consciousness' (p. 25). Because this leads to the suggestion that things can be real only as present, and not as past and future, the time of the created order tends to be evacuated of its significance. The outcome is the apparent implication that only God and the soul have true ontological weight, so that a choice often appears inevitable between idealism and atheism. Only the doctrine of the Trinity enables an escape from the necessity of making that choice, because the triune God is not a sheer point of presence, but one who can make room within himself for the other.

In the second essay, Paul Helm argues that there is a way to read Augustine's account which saves it from Professor Jenson's strictures. He prefaces his account with a robust defence of the traditional Western conception of the relation of time and eternity, and proceeds, in a rather different way from that essayed in a later essay by Alan Torrance, to oppose any application of tenses to the act of divine creation. The 'before' of creation is not a temporal before, and this is shown by the fact that all events in the created world, including the 'big bang' are processes and so involve time. Professor Helm's contention is, therefore, that the universe is beginningless but contingent. Even though creation is in a sense eternal, it does not follow that it is necessary – that it has to exist – and is not therefore the product of free divine willing.

On the strength of this analysis, the author suggests that the apparent contradictions of Augustine's account should be understood in the light of a two standpoint theory. This applies to the doctrine of creation a revised version of Immanuel Kant's doctrine of the two aspects, according to which human action appears to be free according to an internal perspective, determined from an external point of view. The doctrine is an adaptation, because instead of two different temporal standpoints, we have in this case one eternal and one temporal standpoint. 'That temporal order which is the created universe is necessarily to be understood either from a timeless standpoint, as a timeless God understands it, or from a temporal vantage point, as you and I understand it' (p. 35). This means that while from our standpoint creation is continuous creation, from God's standpoint, 'what is created is one temporally extended or ordered universe' (p. 35).

The reader of this volume will find much profit in comparing
this position with that of Alan Torrance below, in that both in
similar, but also significantly different, ways attempt to
maintain the relation within difference of eternal God and
temporal world. Professor's Helm's distinctive way of construing the position is in terms of the way the world is known
or experienced by each of the two – divine and human –
subjects. His argument is designed to evoke an understanding
of what it means to say that the world is, from God's side,
understood by one who, as a subject, stands outside space and
time, and he does this by a sustained engagement with
Augustine's reflections on the nature of time. It is in this
context in particular that Helm calls upon the modified two
standpoint theory, contending that Augustine's apparently
reductionist reflections about the unreality of time should be
understood as a metaphysical and epistemological thesis about
the nature of time from the standpoint of the creature; his more
realistic expressions from the point of view of one who knows
all temporal events timelessly.

Professor Helm's essay is written in defence of a thesis which
has come under attack in recent times, that God is timeless.
That is to say, his treatment of the central question of the
relationship of eternity and time takes it in its most intractable
form: the relationship of the timeless to that which is characterised by time. Another way of putting this would be to
say that he accepts one aspect of the legacy of Greek philosophy
to the Western theological tradition, and he defends the
position in the final section of his paper. Doctrines of divine
timelessness and immutability are true conceptualisations of
the being of the God of the Bible, because they affirm the
actuality of God. To cite the final sentence of the paper: 'The
incarnation is not the achieving of divine fullness, it is the
expression of that fullness which only the timelessly eternal
God can provide' (p. 46).

The question of God's timelessness, and some of its ramifications, will recur in later papers. But first, some other
questions arising from the history of the interrelation of
ancient philosophy and the doctrine of creation must be
treated. As has already been suggested, the meeting of Bible
and philosophy takes a particularly problematic form in the
doctrine of creation, and it is the function of the two following historical papers, both by Colin Gunton, to focus on
earlier and later stages of this syndrome. The first concerns
the interpretation of scripture. One only needs to recall to
mind the controversy surrounding the theory of evolution to
realise that the interpretation of scripture has bulked large in

the controversies surrounding the doctrine of creation. At the centre has always been the first chapters of Genesis, and rightly, for they are of central importance for the doctrine of creation, among other reasons by virtue of their place at the beginning of the canon of scripture. Although it must be borne in mind that they are by no means the only important texts – for those celebrating the place of Christ in creation are surely also of constitutive importance for an adequate theology of creation – they have been at the centre of discussion. In this context, because it is easy to believe that problems with the text are consequent upon modern science, it is important to remind readers that there have always been disputes about the interpretation of this document, and that 'creationism' has never been the mainstream teaching of the Christian tradition.

The narrative form of Genesis has in particular always been an embarrassment to a certain kind of philosophical mind, and it is argued in the first of the two historical papers that the tradition of allegorical exegesis, beginning with the Jewish commentator Philo of Alexandria and continuing through Origen to Augustine and beyond, introduced a form of platonising interpretation that has in the long run detracted from giving an adequate account of the theology of the text. The chief problem is the fact that Platonism makes it difficult to take the text's affirmation of the goodness of material reality and its complex plurality with due seriousness. The argument of the paper is that while the theology of both Origen and Augustine is vitiated by this form of Platonism, so that it prevents them from allowing the Bible to say what it does say, Basil of Caesarea, somewhere midway in time between them, shows evidence of a different theology which modifies his Platonism and allows a more enthusiastic affirmation of material plurality.

The status of the material world is, for Christian theology, very much bound up with the incarnation, the affirmation that in Jesus of Nazareth the Son of God takes part of that world to himself, and, consequently, dies and is raised in order that God should redeem all of it (Ephesians 1.1–10). The second historical study takes up the bearing of this on the doctrine of creation, and argues that the mediaeval treatment of creation is almost entirely devoid of christological content. Part of the problem is the construing of the relation between eternal God and temporal world in terms of causality. While this can be construed personally and in terms of contingency, too often it encourages a conception of the relation of Creator and creation in terms of omnicausality – God being the cause of everything – in such a way that the relative independence of the created order – its *contingency* – becomes endangered. But it is not only the concept of cause that is suspect. The same can equally happen in the case of a shift to creation in terms of will, so that the only way to conceive creation as being both dependent on God and enabled to be itself in that relation is a trinitarian one, which relates both causing and willing to the eternal love of God.

Only with the Reformation, prepared for as it is intellectually in the late mediaeval theories of contingency and free creation, does this dimension come to the fore, though in Calvin the trumpet gives a rather uncertain sound. Luther's trinitarian reading of the first chapter of Genesis is striking, as are some of Calvin's accounts of the work of the Spirit in creation. The problems for Calvin come with his concern, in his treatment of providence, so to stress the omnicausality of God that the mediating functions of the Son and the Spirit retreat into the background. In face of this, what is needed, it is argued, is a more adequate conception of the mediation of creation, specifically a trinitarian one, in which due weight is attributed to the forms of activity of both Son and Spirit in achieving the will of God the Father.

Because of the renewed trinitarianism of the Reformers, one of the features of their teaching was a return to a robust affirmation of the doctrine of creation out of nothing. The same is the case with some of their modern successors. After relative neglect in the nineteenth century, the doctrine was stated in vigorous terms by Barth, a position critically revised in more recent times by Jürgen Moltmann, whose distinctive panentheistic reinterpretation of the doctrine is subjected to a sustained critique by Alan J. Torrance. Its fundamental teaching is that creation is unconditioned – 'a radically free and sovereign act on the part of God'. Moltmann's much-discussed 'kenotic' doctrine of creation attempts to avoid both emanationism and pantheism, on the one hand, and the attribution of the universe's origin to arbitrary divine power on the other. After an outline of Moltmann's adaptation of the kabbalistic doctrine of *zimzum*, which locates the beginning of things in an act of divine contraction, Dr. Torrance asks whether the doctrine achieves what Moltmann wishes it to.

Two chief problems reveal themselves. The first concerns whether Moltmann can state his position without contradiction, or without falling into one of the two pitfalls he sought to avoid. The second arises from the concepts of space and time, and it is contended that Moltmann's attribution of space and time to God is in danger of turning them into absolutes, and so of endangering the very doctrine he is concerned to articulate.

In engaging with these questions, the author draws upon the work of the philosopher D. C. Williams in order to formulate the doctrine of creation out of nothing in such a way that it avoids the kind of entanglement in the tenses of our linguistic tradition that involves attributing time to God. Instead, then, of interpreting 'creation as either located in time or extended in time' we should 'think in terms of God's creating the totality of spatio-temporal identities together with their interconnective matrices from absolutely nothing' (p. 98).

Three advantages are gained from this approach to the doctrine of creation out of nothing. The first is that it avoids a deist conception of creation according to which, because creation is temporally distant from us, we lose any sense of the immediacy of God's present relation to the created order. The second gain is the avoidance of a 'foundationalist' view of things in which creation is more 'original' than christology, which is thus relegated to a secondary theological domain unrelated to the doctrine of creation. Third, this in turn means that the theology of creation can play a more central role in theology. In sum, to affirm the doctrine of *creatio ex nihilo* is also to affirm that 'every facet of creation and every aspect of existence require ultimately to be interpreted in relation to God and therefore in terms of its specific concrete relations to the divine Triunity' (p. 102). The paper ends with a call for a more fully trinitarian construction of the doctrine, and one which would have the effect of implicating ecclesiology in our considerations of cosmology – a conclusion interestingly echoing that of Robert Jenson.

In 'Creation and Eschatology', Professor D. W. Hardy raises the question of eternity and time in a rather different perspective, from the 'end' rather than the 'beginning'. At the heart, here, is 'the nature of the configuration of the world and what occurs there in its trajectory to its outcome' (p. 105). The problem in recent discussions of the topic is that theology has drawn back, partly through fear of science, from consideration of a broad perspective which includes nature and history as well as the new covenant in Jesus Christ. We must then ask afresh: what is creation about? Here two groups of answers are available: the one largely descriptive, the other normative, in terms of the purposiveness of the being of the universe. The danger, however, which is constantly present, is of treating creation as chiefly the background for other, and particularly, human, concerns. What, then, is the point of eschatology in this context? It is similar to the point of talk of creation, in being concerned with the structuring of creation to an end. Once again, however, theologians have here tended to limit their writings to indirect enquiry, as the horizon for the treatment of other issues.

It is the service of science to theology that it enables a more direct engagement with creation and eschatology. But the poverty of such attempts as those of Frank Tipler to engage with them lays on theology the responsibility of considering them in relation to God. Professor Hardy makes a number of points which cumulatively enrich his case. First, while creation is concerned with the establishment of conditions of stability and thus with delaying its ending, eschatology introduces a note of tension which directs creation beyond itself. 'Creation itself is a transcendent constitution whose nature partially eludes those who are within the trajectory from creation to eschatology, and eschatology is a transcendent reopening whose character is similarly partially hidden' (p. 116). Second, because the creation is an order of inter-related particularities, our doctrines may tell us how the universe is a spatio-temporal relational field, but more than that is needed, because account must also be taken of stronger relational fields which involve the conferral of recognition and the scope for freedom on others. Third, then, conceptions of covenant enable this further specifying of interrelationality in terms of such phenomena as disruption and restoration, as in the relations between God and Israel. The advantage of the idea of covenant, which for Christians is realised in Christ, is that it 'recognises the possibility of otherness as gift' (p. 120).

This otherness has to be understood in terms both of stability and mobility, and, further, it has both ontological and moral dimensions. It means that the 'purpose of the world is to fulfil its finitude' (p. 125). It also has implications for our understanding of the being of God. 'The constitution of creation, and its permeation by eschatology, seem to be products of a certain kind of divine gift which constitutes the other as such, and as deserving fulfilment in its own right' (p. 123). But the very otherness of the creation involves the possibility of a radical dislocation, so that the re-establishment of the dynamics of creation requires redemption. The christological centre of this leads to a final section in which the realisation of creation and eschatology in worship is celebrated – yet another allusion to ecclesiological dimensions. It is in worship that the true and free response to creation is realised, and at the same time the dynamic of creation is incorporated in that response. Thus it is that 'Creation and eschatology return glory to God – the very glory they are given through the trinitarian movement of God toward and in them' (p. 133).

The two final papers consider aspects of the human response to divine creation. First, the aesthetic realm is treated by Brian Horne in 'Divine and Human Creativity'. Arthur Koestler's conception of human creativity in terms of bisociative acts – acts in which previously unconnected dimensions of human experience are brought together – is used to argue that the capacity to make something new is distinctively and intrinsically human. Martin Buber developed a similar theme more or less simultaneously, but goes further in suggesting a link between creativity and freedom. Acts of creation – which occur not only in art but in humour and science also – are acts whereby humans transcend the determinism of the natural world.

Reflecting on the neglect of this theme in the history of theology, Dr. Horne wonders whether it is of a piece with the neglect of the doctrine of creation in favour of a concentration on redemption. The notion that this might be related to the image of God in man is almost entirely neglected in the mediaeval era, and indeed, beyond, because of the tendency to limit conceptions of the image to the exercise of reason, not material activity. That things have changed in recent times is demonstrated with a reference to O. C. Quick and a longer engagement with Dorothy L. Sayers. Her employment of the notion of the creative imagination goes back through George MacDonald to Coleridge. But something needs to be added, and for that the author goes to the theology of Eastern Orthodoxy. Sergius Bulgakov sees it to be of the essence of human being to be called 'not only to contemplate the beauty of the world, but also to express it'. Thus, in ways that can be related to Koestler's vision, Bulgakov can be seen to understand the purpose of art as revealing the beautiful that is there but undiscovered in the world around us. For this tradition, art is a part of holiness, and, indeed, has an eschatological significance.

Yet there is an ambivalence in this and other Orthodox aesthetics, and it concerns the status of secular art. Is there no place for that in a theological account? Moreover, in a world broken by sin, it is not enough to conceive art – as Koestler tends to – in terms of the realisation of a subjective vision of reality. Art reveals also a wrestling with intractable existence, so that it must be possible in a theology of aesthetics to incorporate all of the insights that have been reviewed. What is common to them is that they all arise out of our freedom, and that means a positive freedom, such that if we do not create we fall away from the *imago dei* and fail to achieve release from the determinism of the natural order. 'The *possibility* of creation is lodged within the existence in mankind of the image of God; the *necessity* of creation is lodged in our creatureliness as part of the determined material universe' (p. 147).

Even less than we can avoid the call to creativity can we evade the command to be good, so that the collection ends with Christoph Schwöbel's chapter on the dogmatic basis of an ethic of createdness. He begins by warning against an excessive dominance by a current concern, like ecology, because that can falsify the dogmatic relevance of the doctrine of creation by obscuring its chief meaning and bearing. God, not human agents, is responsible for the sustaining and preserving of creation, so that what is called for is an ethic of createdness which is informed by a theology of creation. The heart of the matter is the relation between faith, as the gift of God, and human action as response to that gift.

The shape of the ethic of creation is then spelled out first in a review of the main features of a trinitarian dogmatics of creation. This establishes three main features: the distinction between creator and creation; creation as grounded in the being of God as love, and not merely as the product of will; and creation as a complex act. Having established by this means that the doctrine of creation is concerned with far more than simply answering the question of why there is anything rather than nothing, Professor Schwöbel moves into an examination of the relation between the two meanings of 'creation' in English, the act of creating and the result of that act – creating and createdness. Both meanings are integral to the doctrine of creation.

The outcome of an analysis of creation in this double respect is threefold. First, the absolute giving that is the meaning of the doctrine of creation out of nothing has its complement in creation as contingent. This means both that the world is permanently dependent upon God for its being and that it has the status for us not as given but as gift. Second, the faithfulness of God's giving leads into a doctrine of God's continuing care for the world which is radically different from deist unconcern, and leads to the salvation *of*, not *from*, the world. In this light, the created order, with its combination of structure and spontaneity, can be seen to provide a basis for finite freedom – the proper freedom that pertains to the creature. And third, the orientation of creation to the glory of God – the triune mutuality of communicating and communicated glory, not a glory of individual self-regard – indicates that neither human utility nor glory is the focus of an ethic of creation. Thus are excluded the anthropocentric approaches to ethics which have done so much harm in our relations with the rest of the created world. In contrast to them, the shape which a Christian ethic of creation will take is, finally, indicated by a demonstration of the relation of the doctrine of creation to the presuppositions and the norms of human action, and their relation to the Kingdom of God as the Highest Good. The chapter concludes with an argument that it is in prayer that the relation between God's action and ours is grasped, and thus the essential shape of human action discerned.

The writers presented in the following pages are not in complete agreement in their treatment of the details of their cases, and, indeed, when it comes to understanding that most central topic, the relation of eternal and infinite God to the temporal and spatial universe, there are some considerable differences. And yet the chapters, together, do not present a chaos of individual offerings, but a communal effort in which there are many agreements and enriching overlaps. As has been noted, several of the authors indicate something of the relation of the doctrine of creation to the life and worship of the church, as she, in obedience to Colossians' vision of Christ the mediator of creation who, as such, is 'the head of the body, the church' (Colossians 1.15–18), engages with 'the world' that is both hostile to its maker and the object of his creating and redeeming love. Overall, however, the hope is that together we shall have offered an insight into the importance of the dogmatic content of the doctrine of creation, and suggested opportunities for further thought and research.

1. Aspects of a Doctrine of Creation

Robert W. Jenson

I

The Bible begins with a straightforward statement of doctrine: 'In the beginning God created the heavens and the earth.' Westermann has established this as the right translation, by showing that Genesis 1.1 is the caption of what follows. Resistance to Westermann's insight, and translations that make the first line a dependent clause, derive from residual prejudices of an earlier mode of critical exegesis, that always found the 'real' text, and so the proper meaning of the canonical text, in some stage of the text before and so outside the structure of the canonical text.

Early Judaism recognised Genesis' proposition as authoritative teaching. So the mother of 2 Maccabees 7.28, invoking the minimum faith for the sake of and with the support of which her son was to be martyred: 'I beg you, my child, to look at the heavens and the earth . . . and acknowledge that God made them . . .'. The primal church simply took over the Jewish teaching. For her the doctrine of creation was received truth that did not need to be asserted, but functioned rather as a warrant in asserting other things. Thus the absolute difference between Creator and creature is an automatic classification (Romans 1.25; Hebrews 4.3). 'Creator' is simply equivalent to 'God' (1 Peter 4.19), and 'creature' is simply equivalent to 'everything' (Romans 8.19–39; Colossians 1.23). *Anthropine ktisis* can mean 'human person' (1 Peter 2.13).

Indeed, even what the New Testament *does* explicitly state as doctrine, that creation is done through and for Christ, is not independent new teaching. Contemporary Judaism taught that '. . . it was for us that thou didst create the world . . .' (II Esdras 6.55); and the primal church simply took over this claim also: e.g. 'for the church's sake the cosmos was framed' (Hermas, *Vision* II.4.1). Since it is Christ's death and resurrection that create the church, the doctrine of Colossians is simply a straightforward conclusion: 'All things were created through

him and for him . . .', precisely as 'He is the head of . . . the
church . . .' (Colossians 1.15–20).

Only in the course of the second century does creation again
become an explicit matter of theology. Notoriously, this occurs
in the church's confrontation with various philosophical or
mythological denials that the one responsible for this world
can be the good God and Father of Jesus Christ. So Justin
against Marcion, who, according to Justin, wants us 'to regard
another as greater than God the Creator . . .' (*First Apology*,
29).

Since these second- and third-century conflicts are contemporaneous with, and indeed part of the reason for the church's
great initial spurt of creed-making, explicit recognition of the
biblical doctrine as dogma occurs so soon as there is any
dogma at all. The 'rules of faith' of the earliest fathers insist
on it; so, for example, Tertullian, before 200: 'The rule of faith
unique . . . and irreformable, namely that we are to believe
in one God Almighty, Creator of the world . . .'. So do the
baptismal creeds, as the third-century creed of Caesarea: '. . . in
one God, Father, Pantocrator, the Creator of all things visible
and invisible'.

Finally it is to be noted that what is thus established as a
rule of faith and an essential item of the creed is simply the
biblical assertion itself, against the rather straightforwardly
contrary views of pagan antiquity.

II

But what indeed is thus asserted? What does 'create' mean?
Notoriously, scripture reserves the verb *BRH* for one use only,
to refer to God's creative act. Just so, of course, the usual lexical
devices help little in determining its meaning. This is perhaps
no great problem. If Genesis 1.1 is a caption, then the meaning
of *barah* in Genesis 1.1 is in any case defined by the story the
caption summarises. It is therefore to the story itself we must
turn. That the doctrine of creation is at least initially developed
as exegesis of Genesis 1, is of course a venerable strategy
indeed.

Point one. There *is* indeed other reality than God, and it is
really other. The rhetorical drum-beat of Genesis 1 is itself the
chief means of its teaching, and primary among the repeated
rhythms is 'And God said "let there *be*. . . ." And there *was*. . .
(*yehi . . . weyehi . . .*)'.

The point is by no means obvious. In the world's high
cultures, the dominant understanding of our being and the
being of our world is that it derives from a divine world by

creation or emanation or in the fashion of a conclusion from premises, so that in the last analysis there is no reality truly *other* than the divine, but only extensions or diminutions of the divine. And indeed once the church was properly involved in a high culture other than Judaism, the point became a struggle also for believers. Thus, for a central instance, the entire Arian controversy can be seen as the final expulsion from Christian thinking of the continuous spectrum of being which pagan antiquity posited from deity itself down through the ranks of diminishing images.

Point two. That there is other reality than God depends entirely on his will. 'God said, "*let* there be. . . ." And there was . . .' That God or the gods evoke other reality by speaking is not peculiar to Israel. What *is* characteristic of Israel's understanding of the world is *what sort* of word God speaks to bring the world to pass: he utters a command, this is obeyed, and the obeying act is the existence of the world. *Torah* and righteousness are the very being of reality other than God.

Israel thus understands the reality of the world on the pattern of her own reality. Also this formal pattern is not peculiar to Israel. What is peculiar is her actual understanding of her own reality; we will return to this point in a moment.

Point three. All the above holds precisely in the present tense. The world at any moment would not be did not God will it. Therefore there is one sense – and I am going to insist that it is indeed but *one* sense – in which the dependence-relation between the world and God is as such independent of the difference between one moment of created time and another. Two recurring problems of the theology of creation will appear as we work through this point, that I will note as we come to them, one to solve on the spot and the other to save for later.

Genesis sets the world's dependence on God's will in the present tense in that it asserts this dependence by stories that are aetiological in their form: the stories are told as certification of our life as we now live it and our world as we now find it. If I may put it so, though their locutionary content is past events, whose reality as past and as events we are to take with full seriousness, their illocutionary object is the problematic character of the present moment.

The Old Testament exegesis that found aetiologies every-where and thought it was finished when it had done so, is of course now discredited. But the quite specifically aetiological character of Genesis 1–11, that is, of precisely the part of the biblical narrative in which God's partner is the world and the human race as such, is surely plain. And that it is *this* part of the biblical narrative of which this must be said brings us the first and easier of those problems.

It has often been supposed that the doctrine of creation is that part of Christian teaching which can be shared with the otherwise unbelieving. It is now widely understood that this is not the case. But nevertheless it seems plain that there must be something in the common opinion, in that all cultures, high and low, early and late, tell stories of the kind that appear in Genesis 1–11, and around a quite limited set of motifs. What is common to all the race, I suggest, is a set of *worries*. Thus technology is felt as a spiritual force in every culture that becomes aware of it, as is the ambiguity of that force; and so there is regularly a story of the first technologist, in Genesis a very touchy fellow indeed. The stories of Genesis 1–11 are told to certify present reality.

Now – among the universally-felt fragilities of existence, one is peculiar. For not only is our human world problematic in its historically developed features, but so also is the pre-condition of our historical world, the world in its sheer givenness, prior to all we do in and to it. There is, as it were, an absolute worry. Why this world instead of some other? Indeed, 'Why is there anything at all? Why not rather just nothing?'

The absolute worry differs from all others in one decisive respect. The problematic character of metallurgy can be mastered by stories of human motivations and actions, the problematic character of the world as such cannot. It is thus not so much fragility that we here confront as it is *mystery*.

Therefore throughout the cultures there are stories that begin 'When there was still no world . . .', or 'When everything was nothing . . .'. Genesis begins precisely so with its second verse.

This is of course a logically very peculiar sort of narrative beginning. For to recount the beginning of everything, we have to start by talking about how things were before that beginning; but of course it is the beginning of *everything* we are now trying to narrate. This peculiarity can raise the other recurring theological problem, in fact already signalled: Is the fact stated by 'God creates the world' truly an event or must the proposition be read as stating a timeless relation? As already noted, it is always true that now the world depends on God's will. That creation is told by a *story* necessitates reference to the situation before the story's first event, yet the whole point of *this* story is that there was nothing before this event.

When the creation story is mythic, this occasions no problem: the story then does not by its inner intention narrate any single event but a permanent structure of all events. And there has been recurrent pressure on Christian theology in fact to read Genesis as myth, whether or not under that label.

Thus the great Origen was clear on the dogma: 'First, that God is one, who created and ordered all things, who when there was nothing made the universe to be . . .'.[1] But interpreting the dogma, he identifies God as a 'benevolent and creative energy (*dynamis*)', and is promptly in trouble. For 'to think that such energies of God were ever . . . idle would be as absurd as impious'.[2] Then must we not conceive God as timelessly creating, and the creature as always existing? Origen seems to have come up with various solutions, none satisfactory to him.

In modern theology, the pressure to think of creation as a standing relation has intensified; the only recently defunct 'process theology', for example, with its usual simplicity of mind, simply denied that creation is an action. Augustine had a bad case of the problem. He confesses, 'And so in the Word that is co-eternal with you, you instantaneously and eternally say all that you say, and bring to pass what you say . . . , but nevertheless not all the things you make by your speaking occur simultaneously and eternally', and can offer no resolution of the 'nevertheless'.[3]

Point four. The reality other than God has an absolute beginning. The creation story is not in fact mythic, for it does not make the creature antecede itself, it does not tell us anything *about* what the creature was like when it was still not anything. Augustine states the case precisely: 'You have made all times; and before all times you are, nor in any time was there not time.'[4] Were the nothingness of the creature before it exists something describable, a chaos-being, then God's act to create the world would be, like Marduk's, a victory over this chaos, or, like Father Time's act, an impregnating of it. But however such myth may provide Israel with ritual or literary motifs, the narrative assertion itself is sedulously avoided; as of course it must be since the Lord is above all a jealous God, brooking no competitive forces or consorts.

Does Genesis then teach creation *ex nihilo*? Judaism, anyway, read it so. Thus the Maccabees citation continues, '. . . and not from anything existent (*ouk eks onton*)'. And this very passage seems indeed to be quoted, if with antique freedom, by Hermas as the first and foundational item of his rule of faith:

[1] Origen, *Peri Archon*, 1.2–8, 10.
[2] Origen, *Peri Archon*, 1.4.3.
[3] Augustine, *Conf*, 11.7.10.
[4] Augustine, *Conf*, 11.14.17.

'First of all believe, that there is one God who created the universe and made the universe to be from having not been (*ek tou me ontos eis to einai*).' Sometimes by way of Hermas and sometimes directly from Maccabees the reading is quoted by Irenaeus,[5] Origen[6] and so on.

It seems to me, moreover, that this Jewish-early Christian exegetical tradition was right. Genesis 1.2 evokes pre-creation entirely with negatives, except for describing the presence of the '*ruach* of the Lord'. Most of the exegetes whom I usually follow read 'wind from God', but I cannot follow them. Whatever may have been said in traditions from which the priestly writers drew, it is quite inconceivable that the shapers of the *canonical* text can have written *ruach Elohim* and not thought of 'God's Spirit'.

So according to Genesis, certainly as Judaism and the church have read it, before there is the creature, there is God and nothing. And this nothing is not the kind that can be the antecedent of something. God and only God is the creature's antecedent.

Point five. Reality other than God has not only a beginning but a termination. If I may use a term not itself found in Genesis 1 but assuredly capturing its spirit, reality other than God is 'flesh', of which it must be said, 'My spirit shall not abide in mortals forever, for they are flesh . . .' (Genesis 6.3).

Also this termination must be either nothingness or God. And here the end might perhaps indeed be a sort of real nothingness. The creation once given, there may perhaps be a sense in which a creature's return to nothingness could be its entry into a Negation. However that may be, the end held out in Genesis is not *das Nichtige* but God.

In Genesis creating is a purposive act. The motif of creation by manufacture, obviously present in the traditions the priestly writer took up, is rigorously subordinated to creation by speaking. That speaking – as we have noted – is command, and the up-beat to the downbeat 'God said' is 'and it was good'. It is vital to grasp that in Genesis' story also the 'and it was good' belongs to the creative act itself: things are *in that* they are judged good by God. *Tov* in Hebrew works just like 'good' in English: it says 'good *for*' something. Things are good in that God judges that they are good for his purposes.

Why is there anything at all? Genesis' answer may now be stated: the world is good in that it has been commanded to be good for the intent of the commander.

[5] Irenaeus, *Against the Heresies*, IV.20.2.
[6] Origen, *Peri Archon*, I.3.3; II.1.4, and elsewhere.

And Genesis also makes clear what the world's purpose is. Israel used and invented primal aetiologies in her own way: she incorporated them in a total narrative whose defining event is not the Beginning but an event within what is begun, the Exodus. The genealogies of Genesis 1–11 are the very point of the chapters: they establish the sequence of connected events from the 'genealogy' of the universe itself to Abraham and the other patriarchs. But already the patriarchal history is itself a prelude, of a remarkable sort: the patriarchal history tells how God was the God of Israel before there was Israel. Before God created Israel by leading her out of Egypt to Sinai and Canaan, Israel existed as those to whom God *promised* that there would be Israel.

Thus the unitary history of Israel's own 'creation' is a history of promise, of the leap-frogging mutuality of prophecy and event. It is into this history that the genealogies incorporate the general history of humankind. And it is into the universal history thus posited that Genesis 1–2 incorporate also 'the beginning'. So we may finally state fully the particular way in which Israel participated in humankind's general worry about being, and in humankind's story-telling way of meeting that worry: what Israel certifies for the present by its telling of the beginning is the absolute scope and validity of the promises to Israel.

Point six. If all this last is true then the initial posit that God is our end cannot simply mean that we have God as our boundary – after the manner of, perhaps, Barth's *Romans*. According to the gospel, in the most perfect dramatic continuity with Genesis, it is Christ as head of the church and the church as the body of Christ that is the purpose for which the creation is 'good'. One could derive the whole Chalcedonian doctrine – in, I think, its neo-Chalcedonian development – from this proposition, but here let me work the other way around and presume the classic christology.

God is our end in that God the Son, himself 'one of the Trinity', is identified with a human community, the church, and in that the fulfilment of this identification is the purpose of our being. That is, God is our end in that we will be taken into the triune life. *Deification* is our end.

III

How now are these dogmatic propositions to be accommodated systematically? Let me begin by quoting John of Damascus: 'He creates by thinking, and what is thought comes actually to subsist as a work carried on by the Logos and perfected by the

Spirit.'[7] I am not concerned to commend the details of John's doctrine, but its pattern. Creation is said to become actual (*hyphistatai*) as an *ergon*, a work; and this work is done as it is enveloped in all temporal dimensions by the three persons God is. God the Father is the sheer given of creation, in John's material doctrine as a consciousness for which the creature is a thought. This thought is real in that it is perfected by God the Spirit, and in that it is carried along by God the Son.

Another citation, that will be familiar to some of you: '. . . the only satisfactory account of the relation between creator and creation is a trinitarian one. . . . The key to the matter is . . . the capacity for us to understand the relation between God and the world as a matter of free relatedness. It is because God the Father creates through the Son and Spirit . . . that we can conceive a world that is both real in itself, and yet only is itself in relation to its creator.'[8] If we are thus to say that creation is a relation to Father, Son and Spirit *and* to remember that these three are real only in their relations to each other, we arrive again at the idea of envelopment: to be a creature must be to be involved in some way in the mutual life of the triune persons. We are, using John's language again, worked out, *ergon hyphistatai*, *among* the three.

I can now jump to my central assertion, which is merely the converse of these considerations: for God to create is for him to open a place in his triune life for others than the three whose mutual life he is. John of Damascus again: 'God is . . . his own place'.[9] In that place, he *makes room*, and that act is the event of creation.

This place in the triune life we call 'time'. That creation is above all the making of time for us, is of course again an ancient insight, most famously exemplified in Book XI of Augustine's *Confessions*, where the passion to understand God's creating turns out to have as its content the one question, 'What is time?' My answer: created time is room in God's own life.

If creation is God's making room in himself, then God must be *roomy*. I have elsewhere argued that this roominess of God should be thought of as *his* 'time', that God's eternity is not his immunity to time but his having all the time he needs.[10] As God is the Father, he is Source, *arche* to God; as God is the

[7] John of Damascus, *The Catholic Faith*, 6.6–8.
[8] Colin Gunton, *Christ and Creation* (Carlisle: Paternoster Press and Grand Rapids: Eerdmans, 1993), p. 75.
[9] John of Damascus, *The Catholic Faith*, 13.9–11.
[10] Robert W. Jenson, *Essays in Theology of Culture* (Grand Rapids: Eerdmans, 1995), pp. 190–201.

Spirit, he is Goal, *telos*, to God; and as God is the Son, he is
meeting and reconciliation of Source and Goal to be one God.
We have two linguistic options. We can call this structure in
God God's 'time', and so use the word analogously, with God as
primary analogate and the created phenomenon as secondary
analogate, as we do when we use such words as 'good' and
'being' theologically. Or if we are shy about such language, we
can use different words for the two, perhaps adopting something like Barth's coinage of 'pure duration', *reine Dauer*, for
God's case and reserving 'time' for ours. To my present point, it
makes little difference.

Whichever linguistic choice we make, there is in God what I
would like to call – and precisely not as a figure – *dramatic
distention*. So doing I am of course taking up and playing
with the definition of time by the most famous of my predecessors in the strategy of this chapter, in the great chapter
of his *Confessions* to which I have already referred. 'We see
therefore that time is a kind of "distention" (*quandam esse
distentionem*).'[11] Indeed, to make clear what difference is made
by a thoroughly trinitarian understanding of God's creating, I
want to spend a few minutes contrasting Augustine's doctrine
with that here proposed.

In our chapter, Augustine interprets God as sheer Presence,
that is, as sheer timeless consciousness. 'If the present
remained always the present and did not pass into being past,
it would not be time but eternity (*praesens autem si semper
esset praesens nec in praeteritum transiret, non iam esset
tempus sed aeternitas*)' (14.17). 'You, God, *are* eternity' (1.1).

This has the consequence, since what God is defines what it
means to be, that future things and past things cannot be real
as past or future; pasts and futures can be real only as they are
somehow present. 'It is not strictly correct to say, "There are
three modes of temporality: past present and future." It would
be more strict to say, "There are three modes of temporality:
the presence of past things, the presence of present things, and
the presence of future things" (*praesens de praeteritis, praesens
de praesentibus, praesens de futuris*)' (20.26).

Now this situation poses no problem for the infinite
Presence, for whom all things 'are' in just this way, from whom
the past and future are timelessly present. But the question
was: quid sit *tempus*? What about a finite presence? On the one
hand, 'If the present remained always the present and did not
pass into being past, it would not be time but eternity.' And on
the other hand, 'If the present, in order that there be time,

[11] Augustine, *Conf*, 11.29.

must pass into the past, how can it be said to be?' (14.17). Here is the point illustrated – no more – by the chapter's most famous argument (15.20): there can be a *temporal* present tense only as a geometrical point, which is to say, only as itself a temporal nullity. And throughout our chapter, Augustine is continuously on the verge of saying indeed that the question, 'What is time?' can only be answered *'Nihil'*.

Augustine's solution to this dilemma is the human *anima*. Since the soul is the image of the infinite Presence, all things, past and future must somehow be there for it.

But they cannot be there for it in their own entity as they are for infinite Consciousness; for the soul is itself a point on the time line, so that for it past and future really *are* past and future, which is to say, non-existent. It is a general rule: the true realities are 'the presence of past things, the presence of present things, and the presence of future things'. But this works out differently for infinite and finite consciousness: while for God this means that things are present to him in their own entity, for us it means simply 'There are neither future things nor past things . . .' (20.26).

There is just one possibility: past and future can be there for the soul *as* they appear *within* the soul in the soul's own essential presentness. The just cited passage continues: 'Therefore they are in the soul . . . , and I can see no other location for them: the presence of past things is memory, the presence of present things is direct apprehension, the presence of future things is expectation' – *memoria*, *contuitus* and *expectatio* all being, of course, *present* moments.

In this fashion, the soul becomes an ontological oddity indeed: a point with an inside. But if there is to be time – *that is, if there is to be creation* – this is the only possibility left to Augustine. Which is why then, finally, Augustine's notorious word, *'distentio'*, with its suggestion of *distortion*, is metaphysically precise. As my 'present intention' draws expected things into remembered things (27.36), 'the life of this . . . act is distended in memory . . . and expectation . . .' (28.38).

Time can be real only as *distentio animi*. And creation becomes the setting of images of divine sheer Presence, bloated by their lack of divinity.

The legacy of Augustine's description of God's act of creation has been, I think, unfortunate. Time is undoubtedly some sort of extension – and why not say *distentio*? The question is, of what?

Since Augustine, only two doctrines have appeared possible. One is Augustine's own, that time is the extension of the soul. This doctrine keeps God and the soul in the picture, but constantly threatens to dissolve the otherness of the world out there, in a fashion foreign indeed to Genesis. The other is the simple opposite of Augustine's doctrine, that time is a sheer metric of the world out there. This doctrine eschews idealism by falling to atheism. The two appear in their mutual inadequacy ever and again, most recently as the unreconciled interpretations of time within quantum theory and relativity theory.

Time – I think – indeed posits a *distentio*. Only one insight avoids the fatal choice posed to Augustine and by him to Western thought. The *distentio* that enables time is a *distentio not* of finite persons but precisely of *God*. I hinted with the phrase 'dramatic distention'. Father, Son and Spirit are identities who between them make a drama, the complex *energeia* that the living God *is*. There is dramatic narrative, with its *extension* of complication, crisis and resolution, that is the truth of God in himself. Nor is the drama that is in God – that is God – a mere spectacle. It is authentic drama; it has dialogue; it is a moral enterprise between free persons. When the fathers exegeted 'Let us make man' as trinitarian dialogue, they correctly described the event Genesis reports.

The triune God is precisely not a sheer point of Presence, not even the one at the centre of the turning circle from which all things are equally present. And therefore, whether we want to talk about God's 'time' or not, creation is not a problem for God and the posit of time imposes no strain on the character of being. God is roomy; he can make room in himself if he chooses; if he so chooses the room he makes we call time; and that he creates means that he so chooses.

Time, therefore, is *both* the inner horizon of conscious life, as in Augustine and Kant, *and* the external horizon or metric of cosmic events, lived or not, as in Aristotle and all once-born thinkers. For time is in the supreme conscious life, God, and just so is the enveloping horizon of all events that are not God.

IV

And now, finally, back to that list of what is asserted when 'God creates heaven and earth' is asserted.

There *is* other reality than God, and it is really other. The only reliable otherness is that of persons engaged in a discourse that is not merely first and second person, I and Thou. Creatures exist as additional participants and staging within the dramatic dialogue of the Trinity. Just so, they are truly other.

This dependence holds in the present tense also of created time, without thereby being a timeless relation, in that one of the three has his own individual entity, his hypostasis, *within* created time, is one of those among whom and upon whom creatures' participation in God's story is being worked out. The envelopment of our time by God is itself worked out in the course of our time.

God and only God is the creature's antecedent. There is the Father, and he is not as Father more Creator than is the Son or the Spirit. He is the absolute antecedent, as the *arche* of Son and Spirit, and *so* of the space that Father, Son and Spirit open in their life to be our home.

God and only God is the creature's future. God the Spirit is God's own future, and so draws those for whom God makes room to God. And God can be the creature's future, without absorbing the creature, in that God is not a monad: we can be brought into his life while becoming neither Father nor Son nor Spirit. God can himself be the purpose of his own act to create, without absorbing or abolishing his creation, in that God who is his own future is another person than God who has this future.

V

This is not a whole doctrine of creation. It is as much of one – and rather more than that – as one essay will accommodate.

2. Eternal Creation: The Doctrine of the Two Standpoints

Paul Helm

This paper is the second of a pair which explore various aspects of the idea of timelessly eternal creation. The first of the pair[1] is devoted to considering metaphysical objections to the concept of eternal creation, objections particularly from the point of view of those who conceive of God as existing in time. In this paper I shall assume the coherence and meaningfulness of the idea of timeless creation, and try to take an understanding of the idea of timeless creation a stage further, by exploring some of its consequences. As the subtitle of the paper indicates, I aim to argue that we cannot gain any appreciable understanding of the idea of timeless creation of the world in which we live without employing a version of what I have called (with apologies to both Immanuel Kant and Thomas Nagel) the doctrine of the two standpoints. But before I get on to this, which will form the bulk of the second half of the paper, I shall consider some more basic confusions which bedevil our understanding of creation, and of timeless creation in particular. But before I can attempt even this I must sketch what I take the idea of timeless creation to be.

I

To say that God exists timelessly, and that he has created the entire material universe, means that for God there is no past, present and future, that he has created the universe *cum tempore*. There was no time when the universe was not. I stress the negative aspect of this doctrine; God exists time*less*ly. Certain contemporary writers, such as Eleonore Stump, Norman Kretzmann and Brian Leftow, who have provided valuable service in helping to defend the idea of divine timelessness, have also insisted that God's timeless eternity

---

[1] Paul Helm 'Eternal Creation', *Tyndale Bulletin*, November 1994.

has some of the features of temporal *duration*. In this they have followed an important strand in the tradition going back to Boethius. But this emphasis seems to me to be confused. For if divine timelessness is a duration, then it makes sense to ask duration-type questions of the divine life, and the very purpose, or one central purpose, of introducing divine timelessness must be abandoned. So – at the cost of a certain amount of agnosticism – I stress the negative feature of timeless eternity.

It does not follow from the idea of a timelessly eternal Creator that the universe exists necessarily, since it exists by the free choice of its Creator; but it may follow that it exists eternally. I shall say more about this distinction, between existing necessarily and existing eternally, later on. A timelessly eternal God brings about changes in the universe not by himself changing, but by eternally willing changes; as Augustine put it, God does not change his will, he wills a change. I am quite content to suppose that in talking about a timeless God causing the universe we are using 'cause' in an unusual sense, but not I think a sense that is so stretched that it makes no sense. Indeed, if we substitute for 'causes' the expression 'brings about' then I would argue that if a timelessly eternal God brings about the universe he does so in as unqualified a way as a surgeon brings about healing.

It might be asked, why all the fuss? In the face of the fact that hostility to the idea of divine timeless eternity is almost unanimous, why is it important to uphold it?

What are the theological attractions of timelessness as applied to God? There are a number. To many, the idea that God is subject to the vicissitudes of temporal passage, with a part of his life irretrievably over and done with, is incompatible with divine sovereignty, perfection and with that fullness of being that is essential to God. More specifically, by employing the idea of timelessness it is possible to articulate the distinction between the Creator and the creature and to make clear that divine creation is a unique metaphysical action, the bringing into being of the whole temporal order, not the creation of the universe by one who is already subject to time. God creates every individual thing distinct from himself. Finally, for Christians, the affirmation of God's timeless eternity appears to be necessary in order to provide the conceptual materials for affirming the eternal begetting of the Son by the Father.

For if God is in time then any of his actions, such as the act of begetting, is in time, and thus it follows that, if God the Father begets the Son, the Son is begotten in time and that there is a stretch of time, in principle measurable, between the time when the Son was begotten and the time when the material universe was.

So much then, for preliminaries. I wish now to consider some confusions that arise in connection with creation, and especially with timeless creation.

II

Firstly, we tend to confuse science with metaphysics. God's creation of all that is ('the universe') is not a scientific event, like the exploding of a star or the splitting of an atom, nor a series of such events; nor is it a unique historical event, like the Battle of Hastings or the Coronation of the Queen. It is the bringing of the universe into being from a standpoint outside it. For this reason the idea that God exists (timelessly) 'before' the universe cannot mean that God exists temporally before. He exists before, I argue, in the sense in which the Queen exists before the Prime Minister, age comes before beauty, or duty comes before pleasure. These 'befores' are not temporal 'befores', but 'befores' of another kind of priority, betokening a constitutional or hierarchical arrangement. So it is, it seems to me, in the case of the eternal Creator and the creation. There was no time when the Creator was not, any more than there was a time when the creation was not. And yet the Creator exists 'before' the creation. So, I believe, we may interpret the apostolic claim that Christ is before all things (Colossians 1.17).

As John Polkinghorne has recently put it:

> Theology is concerned with ontological origin and not with temporal beginning. The idea of creation has no special stake in a datable start to the universe. If Hawking is right, and quantum effects mean that the cosmos as we know it is like a kind of fuzzy spacetime egg, without a singular point at which it all began, that is scientifically very interesting, but theologically insignificant. When he poses the question, 'But if the universe is really completely self-contained, having no boundary, or edge, it would have neither beginning nor end: it would simply be. What place, then, for a creator?', it would be theologically naive to give any answer other than: 'Every place – as the sustainer of the self-contained spacetime egg and as the ordainer of its quantum laws. God is not a God of the edges, with a vested interest in boundaries. Creation is not something he did fifteen billion years ago, but it is something that he is doing now.[2]

The thought that the Big Bang (or somesuch) might be the first moment of creation rests upon a confusion, that between

[2] John Polkinghorne, *Science and Christian Belief* (London: SPCK, 1994), p. 73.

inaccessibility and nothingness. It may be (here I defer to the authorities) that events prior to the Big Bang are scientifically inaccessible; perhaps presently inaccessible, perhaps always. But if they are this does not confer on the Big Bang the honour of being the act of creation. For the Big Bang was a process; a short, sharp process, but a process nonetheless. For in the Bang pre-existing stuff was involved, however currently inaccessible to scientific articulation that stuff is. The Big Bang was the first imaginable, or first at present imaginable, or first record-able, re-arrangement of pre-existing stuff. As such it is not a candidate for the title of 'act of creation *ex nihilo*'.

So we ought not to confuse creating with making. Existing stuff is necessary for making; hence making is an activity that is temporally measurable; it is a process, which takes so long, and which may be achieved quickly or slowly. And so divine creating is not making, unless we draw our theology from the craftsman-creator of Plato's *Timaeus* ('The construction of the world used up the whole of each of these four elements. For the creator constructed it of all the fire and water and air and earth available, . . .'[3]) rather than from Genesis 1.1.

Because we confuse making and creating, there is a common tendency, across a broad theological spectrum, to think of creation as a process, which it cannot be. Processes can only occur as changes to what is created. (Neither the sequence of days in Genesis 1 (as interpreted by some) nor the theory of evolution by natural selection are possible modes of creation, but of change and development.)

Secondly, as I hinted earlier, there is a tendency to confuse time with contingency. Scripture implies, if it does not affirm, the contingency of the universe in two respects; that its existence is not logically necessary (cf. mediaeval debates about the eternity of matter) and that it owes its existence to the agency of God; it depends upon him. But it does not follow from the contingency of the universe in the above senses that there was a time when the world was not; only that there might not have been a universe. The universe is beginningless, without a first event; but it does not follow from that it is not contingent, and if it is contingent then it has a cause, someone (or some-thing) on whom it depends for its entire existence.[4]

Thirdly, there is a temptation to confuse what we are able to conceive with how things must be. Perhaps, for any time t^1

---

[3] Plato, *Timaeus*, translated by Desmond Lee (London: Penguin, 1977), pp. 44–5.

[4] For a fascinating account of one mediaeval debate about this, see Norman Kretzmann, 'Ockham and the Creation of the Beginningless World', *Franciscan Studies* 45 (1985), 1–31.

prior to the present it is possible to conceive an earlier time than t^1. If this is possible, what does it show? What it shows is not that it is possible to establish a moment of creation, but the reverse of this. For any such putative moment it is possible to imagine an earlier moment than that, and so any supposed moment of creation is in indefinite retreat. On the other hand, the fact that we think in these ways goes no way to establishing that the universe is logically necessary, though (from the Creator's standpoint) it is without temporal beginning. Perhaps we must recognise the strongly regulative influence that conceptions of time and space exert on individuals such as ourselves who are themselves necessarily temporal, and spatial. (Whether such regulative procedures recognise regularities objectively present, or construct or impose regularities, is a further interesting philosophical question.)

Finally, and most importantly for the remainder of this paper, there is an inclination to confuse the standpoint of the Creator with that of the creature. (This is a corollary of an earlier-cited confusion.) As noted earlier, from the Creator's standpoint his creation is a whole; it is not a creation in time, but with time. From the standpoint of an intelligent creature the universe is co-eternal with God, for there is no time when the universe is not. For such an agent the universe unfolds as a temporal sequence, with a past, a present and a future. As Augustine himself put it:

> In the first instance, God made everything together without any moments of time intervening, but now He works within the course of time, by which we see the stars move from their rising to their setting.[5]

Insofar as palaeographers and geologists investigate the past, they investigate past phases of what is (from the Creator's standpoint) the one creation. But at no point is their (or anyone else's) empirical investigation of the past going to lead them to a first moment of creation, since every act of investigation is an act in time. But from the divine standpoint the universe is one whole which exists by the will of God.

So I suggest that in articulating the idea of timeless creation it is helpful, if not actually obligatory, to think in terms of two standpoints; an authorial standpoint, the standpoint of a playwright, say; and the standpoint of someone who is an actor in the play; the time of the author's writing of the play is not, perhaps cannot be, the same as the time of the actors' standpoints in the play. A rather different idea of two standpoints is

---

[5] Quoted in E. McMullin (ed.), *Evolution and Creation* (University of Notre Dame Press, 1985), p. 10.

familiar to us from the philosophy of Kant, who argued that human action, for example, may be understood from the standpoint of science, or from the standpoint of agency. That from the first standpoint human action is determined, while from the second standpoint it is free.

Here I do not wish to defend Kant's distinction, but simply to use the idea of two standpoints to elucidate the distinction between a timelessly eternal Creator and a temporal creation.

We may begin to elucidate this idea of the two standpoints by thinking of two physical standpoints. A building may be viewed from more than one standpoint, let us say, from the respective standpoints occupied by two individuals at the same time. But while any building, in order to be viewed, must be viewed from some standpoint, such viewings are contingent in the sense that one viewer, A, could occupy the standpoint of another viewer B, or vice versa, and there is an infinity of such standpoints.

In the case of time, the contingency is a little less obvious than in the case of space, because of the unidirectionality of time. It follows from the unidirectionality of time (and here I am ignoring the possibilities of retrocausation, time-travel and such like) that what has happened cannot now not have happened. Someone living in 1994 could not now take up Napoleon's temporal standpoint (though he could view the Pyramids, say, from exactly the same spatial standpoint as Napoleon did), and perhaps such a person could never have had Napoleon's standpoint (if, say, having a certain genetic history is essential to an individual being the individual that he or she is).

The distinction between the eternal and the temporal standpoint is even more entrenched than that between two temporal standpoints, with even fewer elements of contingency, in that anyone who occupies a temporal standpoint necessarily occupies some definite temporal standpoint or other, and similarly an occupant of the eternal standpoint has no choice. If God is timelessly eternal then he is necessarily so, and he could not occupy any temporal standpoint; and no temporal creature could be timelessly eternal. For to be temporal is to change, or at least possibly to change, while to be timelessly eternal is necessarily not to change and so not to be able to change. So it is necessarily the case that God, if he is timelessly eternal, cannot translate his eternal standpoint into ours, nor we, creatures of time, translate ours into his.

Of course if God is trinitarian then in addition to the one eternal divine standpoint each person of the Godhead has his own eternal standpoint *vis-à-vis* the other persons of the

Trinity, and if God is necessarily trinitarian then the Son necessarily has the standpoint that he does over against those of the Spirit and the Father. Each of the trinitarian standpoints is eternal. And if the doctrine of the incarnation is true then the eternal Son of God is in the closest possible union with what changes, while not himself changing, and the other persons of the Trinity continue to enjoy a timelessly eternal standpoint *vis-à-vis* the incarnate second person. I shall say a word or two more about the incarnation at the end.

Given these necessary truths, and given the reasonable supposition that any standpoint is either temporal or eternal, and that we exist in time and God exists in timeless eternity, it would appear to follow that for a Christian theist there cannot be a standpointless truth of the matter about events and actions in time, any more than there can be standpointless truth of the matter about timeless eternity. That temporal order which is the created universe is necessarily to be understood either from a timeless standpoint, as a timeless God understands it, or from a temporal vantage point, as you and I understand it. There is no third vantage point, and every agent occupies either the one or the other standpoint.

The contrast in the standpoints can be brought out starkly as follows. From our standpoint God's creation is continuously unfolding, it is a *creatio continua*. The state of the universe at time t^1 does not logically necessitate the character nor even the existence of any phase at t^2 or later, even though there are discovered regularities between different past phases, and promised continuations of them, for as long as the created order persists unregenerated. So from our perspective the Creator may be said to be continuously creating the universe, in that there is more universe today than there was yesterday, for the present builds upon and is made intelligible by the past. But from the divine standpoint what is created is one temporally extended or ordered universe.

Was there a time when God was not incarnate in Jesus Christ? Clearly so. Roughly, during all those years that we denominate as 'BC'. But from the standpoint of the timelessly eternal Creator the Lamb was slain from the foundation of the world (Revelation 13.8).

In *The View from Nowhere*[6] Thomas Nagel draws a contrast between two irreconcilable points of view, the external and the internal. Insofar as a person adopts an internal view he is a subject of experience, and what he learns about the world, and

[6] Thomas Nagel, *The View from Nowhere* (Oxford: Oxford University Press, 1986).

does to the world (and what the world does to him) depends upon the place and the time that he occupies in it. Were he to lose this perspective then he would lose his identity as a particular person. To take up an external view, the view from nowhere, he must de-personalise himself and strive to understand the world from no particular place or time, something he can do with only limited success, partly because it is logically impossible to act, even to think, within such a world.

I am suggesting something similar in the case of the Creator God and ourselves. Besides the externalism which Nagel draws attention to, and which we may strive to attain, there is, for the theist, the externalism of God's standpoint. Perhaps we may even say that this objective, external world, insofar as it is accurately discerned by us, corresponds to a fraction of God's standpoint *vis-à-vis* the material universe. Insofar as we understand the world, including ourselves, in this objective or external way, our thought is isomorphic with the thought possessed by God in his eternal vantage point.

God's is not the view from nowhere or nowhen, but the view from his own unique where and when, the where and when of timeless (and spaceless) eternity. For not only are we subjects, God is also a subject, with an epistemic and volitional standpoint, though not a subject of experience in quite the way that we are. God as a subject stands outside space and time, and views his creatures in a way that is best expressed by us in ways which are free from infection by either temporal or spatial indexicals. God's view is not, of course, a literal viewing; nevertheless God has a unique perspective on the world, a perspective necessarily free of temporal and spatial indexicals. And so he does not take up the cognitive standpoint of any one of his creatures more than that of any other.

III

I wish now to support this idea of the two standpoints by means of a rather extensive (in terms of the overall length of the paper) treatment of an aspect of Augustine's famous treatment of time in Book XI of the *Confessions*. I shall argue that Augustine's remarks there make most sense when he is thought of as presenting two different accounts of time, and that these accounts correspond respectively to the temporal and the eternal standpoints. For I claim that there are two accounts of time and eternity jostling together here, and that one can only make overall sense of St. Augustine's treatment of time if one recognises this fact, and carefully separates remarks which treat of time from the human standpoint from remarks which treat it from the divine standpoint.

There are many statements in Book XI of the *Confessions* which are *prima facie* evidence in favour of the view that Augustine denied length to past and future times because either they now no longer exist or do not yet exist, for only the present moment exists. Here are some:

> But who can measure the past which does not now exist or the future which does not yet exist, unless perhaps someone dares to assert that he can measure what has no existence? At the moment when time is passing, it can be perceived and measured. But when it has passed and is not present, it cannot be.[7]

> Thus my boyhood, which is no longer, lies in past time which is no longer. (p. 234)

> When therefore people speak of knowing the future, what is seen is not events which do not yet exist (that is, they really are future) but perhaps their causes or signs which already exist. (p. 234)

> So future events do not yet exist, and if they are not yet present, they do not exist; and if they have no being, they cannot be seen at all. But they can be predicted from present events which are already present and can be seen. (p. 235)

Let us call these, for ease of reference, the 'first quotations'. According to what Augustine is saying here, neither the future yet exists nor the past any longer exists, and so neither can be measured. Only the present exists, because only the present is now. In saying that the past no longer exists Augustine does not mean that the past is unreal in the sense that a work of fiction is unreal. The events of a work of fiction could never be past, present or future; by contrast, for Augustine the past is no longer present, but it has been; the events of the future are not present, but they will be.

But having asserted the present unreality both of the past and the future Augustine, in almost the same breath, says:

> Where did those who saw prophecies see these events if they do not yet exist? To see what has no existence is impossible. And those who narrate past history would surely not be telling a true story if they did not discern events by their soul's insight. If the past were non-existent, it could not be discerned at all. Therefore both future and past events exist. (p. 233)

[7] Page 233. All page references to the *Confessions* are to the translation by Henry Chadwick (Oxford: World's Classics, 1992).

Here Augustine asserts that future and past events do exist. But, he goes on,

> I know that wherever they are, they are not there as future or past, but as present. For if there also they are future, they will not yet be there. If there also they are past, they are no longer there. Therefore, wherever they are, whatever they are, they do not exist except in the present. (pp. 233–4)

Let us call these the 'second quotations'.

We might refer to the doctrine which lies behind both sets of quotations Augustine's 'temporal actualism'. By this doctrine all the times of the actual world are equally actual, but not all times are now present. Only the time picked out by the uttering of 'now' is present.

In support of the view that only the time picked out by the uttering of 'now' is present it is noteworthy that in the discussion of time in Book XI Augustine frequently provides temporal indexical qualifications to temporal uses of 'exists'. It is not that the present absolutely ceases to exist when it becomes past, it *no longer* exists. No longer exists for whom? It no longer exists for those at the present time. It is for these same people that the future does *not yet* exist.

It could perhaps be argued that in the second quotations Augustine is simply putting up a straw-man to be knocked down; that he is raising the possibility that the future and the past exist, in his rhetorical fashion, only later to demolish it with his view that past and future do not exist, but are only (at best) present traces and anticipations. There is some initial plausibility to this suggestion, but I shall argue against it.

In the second quotations, particularly the one quoted last of all, Augustine explicates past and future in terms of the present. In accordance with his fundamental tenet that only what is present exists, he argues that if the future exists it must exist as a present. Further, if 'present' here is a temporal indexical, then clearly if the future exists, it must be possible for someone to refer to it as the present; not to refer to it now as the present, but to refer to it then (future) as the present. And likewise with the past. Past and future exist if and only if someone is able to refer to those times as 'the present'.

Who could do this? There is only one individual who could do this. Earlier in Book XI Augustine stated:

> In the eternal, nothing is transient, but the whole is present. But no time is wholly present. It (viz. the heart that is fixed and stable) will see that all past time is driven backwards by

the future, and all future time is the consequent of the past, and all past and future are created and set on their course by that which is always present. Who will lay hold on the human heart to make it still, so that it can see how eternity, in which there is neither future nor past, stands still and dictates future and past times? (pp. 228–9)

It is only the eternal one to whom all times are present, and the eternal one for Augustine is God himself, who is related to time in the following fashion:

What times existed which were not brought into being by you? Or how could they pass if they never had existence? Since, therefore, you are the cause of all times, if any time existed before you made heaven and earth, how can anyone say that you abstained from working? (p. 229)

It is not in time that you precede times. Otherwise you would not precede all times. In the sublimity of an eternity which is always in the present, you are before all things past and transcend all things future, because they are still to come. (p. 230)

There are two possible ways of interpreting these expressions and to understand this we must refer to two fundamentally distinct ways of referring to time, by treating it either as an A-series or a B-series. On the A-series view of time, time is to be understood from a point within the temporal series; thus expressions like, 'yesterday', 'today', 'now', 'then', are A-series expressions. One can only refer to a particular day as yesterday from a standpoint within time; if 14th September is yesterday, then 15th September is today, and so on. On the B-series view time is to be understood from an a-temporal perspective, by expressions such as *earlier than* and *later than*, *before* and *after*. Thus on the B-series view of time Napoleon's defeat at Waterloo is earlier than Montgomery's victory at El Alamein; the event of the Battle of Waterloo occurs before that of El Alamein. But Napoleon's victory is only in the past from the standpoint of someone who exists later than that date; and only in the future from the standpoint of someone who exists earlier than that date.

One might initially suppose that Augustine was claiming that the timelessly eternal God created the temporal order as an A-series for himself, or from his own standpoint. From that standpoint the past, though it once existed, no longer exists, while the future has yet to exist. In other words, in creating such a series God commits himself to create a succession of presents.

But there is a crucial argument against this supposition; if God had created the temporal order as an A-series from his standpoint, then God would himself be in time, and the same problems about the relation between past, present and future that, according to Augustine, beset human knowers would beset God as well. In addition, as we shall note in more detail later, in one place Augustine explicitly rules out such an account as an account of divine omniscience (p. 245). Finally, Augustine uniformly presents problems about time as problems for himself and for all temporal minds, but not for God; indeed, as problems for us which only reference to the eternal God can solve.

Alternatively it might be supposed that God created the temporal order as a B-series. From the divine standpoint no one moment of the series would be privileged by being present, but as regards presentness, pastness or futurity, all moments would be in exactly the same position, even though some moments would be earlier in relation to others in the series, some later.

I suggest therefore that according to Augustine God created the temporal order, by an eternal act, as a B-series. And yet it is a B-series of a rather special kind, in that every moment of the series is also eternally present to God in identical fashion. Not temporally present, but eternally present to his mind, in rather the way in which the surfaces of two spheres which touch are present at that point. All times are similarly eternally present to God. As Christopher Kirwan says, Augustine's view is that:

> With respect to any time, God knows (atemporally) everything that happens later than that time. We may also safely presume that in Augustine's view God knows all the past and the present in the same sense.[8]

To the temporal actualism of individuals who are in time ('only now is present') corresponds God's eternal actualism ('all times are eternally present to God').

Insofar as Augustine's concern is with the metaphysics of time from the divine standpoint he takes the view that all times are equally real, because all are equally present to the divine mind. But this was not his sole concern. In this part of the *Confessions* he was facing a question about how time is to be thought about from the human standpoint. And for Augustine problems of human knowledge are strongly conditioned by his conviction that the respective positions of Creator and creature are markedly different in that the creature's condition

---

[8] Christopher Kirwan, *Augustine* (London: Routledge, 1989), p. 174.

is necessarily one of change, the Creator's necessarily one of changelessness.

So when Augustine appeals to memory and expectation he is not offering a reductionist approach to the past or future, arguing that they are respectively constructed out of memories or expectations. He is, rather, offering both a metaphysical and an epistemological thesis about what time is from the standpoint of a creature, and how present, past and future are to be known from such a standpoint. In this connection he sharply distinguishes between, for example, the past, which is no longer present, and recollecting and telling our story of the past, which we do from present memories.

Augustine's markedly epistemological concern is brought out in the following way:

> When therefore people speak of knowing the future, what is seen is not events which do not yet exist (that is, they really are future), but perhaps their causes or signs which already exist. In this way, to those who see them they are not future but present, and that is the basis on which the future can be conceived in the mind and made the subject of prediction. (p. 234)

> Certainly if there were a mind endowed with such great knowledge and prescience that all things past and future could be known in the way I know a very familiar psalm, this mind would be utterly miraculous and amazing to the point of inducing awe. (p. 245)

Were Augustine *identifying* our past with our memories, the nature of the past would fluctuate with our memories, and there would be no way of distinguishing between accurate and inaccurate memories and between different pasts. But we have false memories when the past which is allegedly remembered does not correspond with the past as it really is. The past has a wholly determinate character which our memories only ever fitfully and partially capture. As Timothy Sprigge has expressed it,

> The evidence both of memory and of anticipation provide only an indication to us that we have succeeded in doing this. Thus the something which our judgements about the past, when they are true, succeed in identifying and characterising correctly must be the very past events or past states of certain continuants which they state to have occurred.[9]

One way of construing this Creator–creature difference, as regards past, present and future, is to suppose that 'present'

[9] Cf. T. L. S. Sprigge, 'The Unreality of Time', *PAS* 1991–2, p. 8.

and 'exists' are for Augustine elliptical expressions. Something
cannot exist, or be present *simpliciter*, but only for a knower;
and any knower must of necessity either be in time, as
creatures are, or be timeless, as God is. Do the times which are
at present future to us exist, or not? Answer: they exist for
God, for all moments of created time are timelessly real for
him; and they exist for those creatures contemporaneous with
that future moment, for that moment is present to them, but it
is not now present for us. Is the future real, or is it not? Answer:
it is real to God (to whom all times are similarly present),
though not as the future, and it is real for any for whom that
moment is the present moment. However, it is not present for
us now, since it is future, and what is future is not present. So
the Battle of Waterloo no longer exists for us, and the Battle of
Armageddon does not yet exist for us. But Waterloo and
Armageddon each exist for God because each is eternally real
to God, as are all mundane events, and Waterloo existed for
Napoleon at the time when he could truly say 'The Battle of
Waterloo is taking place now'.

For a time to be real is for that time to be related to
someone's (human or divine) present metaphysical position; for
that time to be known, it must be appropriately related to that
person's cognitive powers and activity.

In the last section of Book XI of the *Confessions* (p. 245)
Augustine contrasts two kinds of omniscience. We can call
these temporal and a-temporal omniscience. A temporally
omniscient person would know the past and the future 'by
heart', as Augustine knew a very familiar psalm. At any point
in singing or reciting the psalm he remembers all the words he
has recited, and anticipates all the words he has yet to sing.
Developing this analogy we may ask, are all the words of the
psalm real, or only those that Augustine is at present singing?
Clearly, the words that he is not singing are real; otherwise
how is Augustine going to distinguish between singing a psalm
and improvising one? Similarly, the past is real, and the future,
but each may be said to exist only as present to God, and the
future unfolds as an A-series to those who exist in time, as all
creatures do.

> Just as you knew heaven and earth in the beginning without
> that bringing any variation into your knowing, so you made
> heaven and earth in the beginning without that meaning a
> tension between past and future in your activity. (p. 245)

This being so, it is hard to resist the conclusion that for God
our past and present, being equally present to the mind of God,
exist. And if they exist they must be real.

In considering the text of St. Augustine's *Confessions*, as well as in considering the more general issue of the relation of eternal Creator to temporal creation of which Augustine's writing is a classical expression, it is unsatisfactory to stress one side of the evidence and ignore the other, and to interpret Augustine as a reductionist about past and future, as constructing them out of the present. Some relief from the difficulty is gained by bearing in mind Augustine's concerns to relate issues of time and change not only to the lives of those in time, but also to the eternal life of God.

So I argue that in Book XI of the *Confessions* Augustine was employing two different senses of 'exist'; he was recognising that 'exist' is an elliptical expression, requiring to be completed by either a reference to a creature in time, or to God. In one of these senses, to exist means to be present, in the other, it means to be real, and to be real is not necessarily to be present. Rather it implies and is implied by the idea of being eternally present, present to the mind of the timelessly eternal God. Some past event certainly isn't a reality existing now; it is a reality which exists in a past present, or which exists because eternally real to God as a phase of his creation that is earlier than the phase we call the present. So the past event no longer exists, that is, it does not belong to now; but it belongs in its own time, and is therefore real, belonging to the ordered series of times which comprise the creation and which are eternally known, and so eternally present, to God. It is to be distinguished, for example, from purely fictional time.

IV

I shall end this paper by considering a couple of objections to what I have been trying to say.

The first objection might be put as follows. A crucial objection to Immanuel Kant's doctrine of the two standpoints, according to which from one standpoint an action is free, while from another standpoint it is determined, is that it is a classic case of attempting to have one's cake and eat it; one wants to ask, is a person free, or not? And it is unsatisfactory to say that judged from one standpoint he is, while judged from another he is not. For the Kantian doctrine suggests that there is no one right answer to the question, and we intuitively feel that there must be.

Does my extension or adaptation of the idea of two standpoints share the same fate as Kant's? I should like to think not, for the following reason. Kant's was an attempt to say two different sorts of things about the same subject, a human being;

that one and the same human being was both free and determined; and in Kant's sense of these terms nothing that is free can be determined; hence the feeling of unease. My own suggestion depends crucially upon the idea of two different subjects, eternal God and temporal creatures, with two different standpoints, and also upon saying things about these two subjects that are not contradictory.

Let us suppose that God eternally knows

(1) Helm is writing his paper on 15th September 1994,

and that I know both that

(2) I am now writing my paper today

and that

(3) Today is 15th September 1994

Are the two states of affairs represented by (1) and (2), and by (3) respectively, contradictory or incompatible in some way? It is hard to see how they could be. The state of affairs known by God, and the state of affairs known by me, may or may not be the same state of affairs, but it is hard to see that, if they are not the same state of affairs, they express incompatible states of affairs.

Relativism is the doctrine that truth is relative to a person's position, or set of beliefs, or intellectual context. Is it relativistic in this sense to suppose that it is true for God that he knows that I am writing this paper on 15th September 1994 while I know, on 15th September, that I am writing this paper now? Hardly, for given his knowledge that I am writing this paper on 15th September 1994, and his knowledge of certain other states of affairs, it follows as a matter of logic from what he knows eternally that he knows that when, on 15th September 1994 I know that I am writing this paper, I know that I am writing this paper now.

Philosophers of religion have frequently debated the question of whether a timeless God can know facts in precisely the same sense in which temporal creatures know. If God is timeless, can he know what I am doing now? How can God, who is timeless, know what time it is now? Some say that he cannot, and so cannot be omniscient, since if he cannot know what time it is now then there are truths which he does not know, and cannot know. Some say that God and a creature can know the same truths, but have different ways, necessarily different ways, of expressing these truths. And still others argue that the use of temporal indexical expressions such as 'now', 'then', 'yesterday', 'today' and so on is indicative not of a different mode of knowledge, but of a different kind of know-how. The use of such expressions helps us, creatures in time, to handle temporal concepts, and to find our way around the temporal order in an efficient way, but it does not provide a distinctive kind of knowledge of time. And so what God lacks when he does not know what time it is now is not knowledge but power, in the same way that someone who does not know how to change a bicycle-tyre lacks power.

Which of these various strategems – if any – commends itself to us as a way of coping with the apparent irreconcilability of divine knowledge and human knowledge ought not to affect our attitude to the idea of the two standpoints. For our question is not, does God know precisely what we know, but is God's knowledge of the created order inconsistent with our knowledge of it, inconsistent to the extent that we have to adopt some form of relativism? Why should we think this?

The second objection is more theological. It may be thought that a timelessly eternal God, impassive, immutable, and immobile could not be the God and Father of our Lord Jesus Christ. Ought we not to ditch timelessly eternal immutability along with all other Platonic and Neoplatonic baggage, and, with Karl Barth and many others, to settle for divine constancy instead? Is not God's being in his becoming?

To these sorts of questions there are, it seems to me, two main sorts of answer. I'll risk trying your patience even further by suggesting, in closing this paper, what these answers are.

In the first place, the constancy rightly affirmed by Karl Barth surely requires some ontological grounding. In virtue of what is God constant, and what sort of constancy is this?

Barth says that God's love:

> cannot cease to be His love nor His freedom His freedom. He alone could assail, alter, abolish or destroy Himself. But it is just at this point that He is the 'immutable' God. For at no place or time can He or will He turn against Himself or contradict Himself, nor even in virtue of His freedom or for the sake of His love.[10]

This is well said, but one needs to ask what it is about God that makes these things true. If God could change, then perhaps he is changing, and then the constancy of his promises or of his love cannot be guaranteed. The only guarantee, or if not the only guarantee then a prime candidate for such a guarantee, lies in the immutability of timeless eternity.

[10] Karl Barth, *Church Dogmatics* 2/1, *The Doctrine of God*, translation edited by G. W. Bromiley and T. F. Torrance (Edinburgh: T. & T. Clark, 1957), pp. 494–5.

Secondly, immutability, immobility and all the rest do not signal weakness and insufficiency in God, but the precise opposite, fullness of being. They affirm the actuality of God. It is because of who God is that he cannot be acted upon for the better and does not need to change. Could such a God be the God and Father of our Lord Jesus Christ? Most certainly. For in the incarnation God the Son does not become something that he was not, but assumes humanity into godhead. The incarnation is not the achieving of divine fullness, it is the expression of that fullness which only the timelessly eternal God can provide.

3. Between Allegory and Myth: The Legacy of the Spiritualising of Genesis

Colin E. Gunton

I Allegory and the Text of Genesis

It is – to adapt a well known saying of Coleridge – among the miseries of the present age that it recognises no medium between *Literal* and *Allegorical*,[1] particularly when it comes to the interpretation of the first chapter of the book of Genesis. Francis Watson has recently demonstrated what may be done in the way of a theological interpretation of that much disputed chapter, and two of his points will provide a starting point for this discussion. The first is his robust critique of those who believe that 'modern thought' provides some kind of criterion for what we may derive from this text. This, he says, is to concede too much to 'modern scientistic ideology, with its totalitarian talk of primitive mentalities which we have now outgrown'.[2] The second is his demonstration of the variety – better trinity – of forms of divine action to which the text bears witness, and particularly those aspects of it which show an interaction of God with the material world, which, I believe, is in many ways the clue to the significance of this text for the Christian doctrine of creation. The two points together enable me to make the crucial historical claim underpinning this paper: that embarrassment with the apparently naive and anthropomorphic account of God's involvement with the material creation is by no means a modern phenomenon, and that in certain respects, as D. F. Strauss recognised, an evasion of the text's claims began early in the tradition.[3]

---

[1] Coleridge's own distinction is between literal and metaphorical, and he was making a case for his concept of symbol. That is directly relevant to the case being made here.

[2] Francis Watson, *Text, Church and World* (Edinburgh: T. & T. Clark, 1994), p. 148.

[3] D. F. Strauss, *The Life of Jesus Critically Examined*, translated by Marian Evans (London: SCM Press, 1973), pp. 43f.

There are many ways of defining allegory. Is it the essence
of allegorical exegesis to know more than the text itself – a
form of eisegesis? Or is allegory perhaps that which necessarily
emerges in the attempt to initiate a conversation between
Bible and contemporary interests, in our age scientific ones –
an attempt to find a 'spiritual' interpretation that enables us
to mediate the text in the culture of our day? Much depends
on what is meant by 'spiritual'. If the meaning is in some
way controlled by a reference to God the Spirit, among whose
functions is to relate us to Jesus of Nazareth, the Son of God
made material for us, there is little objection. But 'spiritualising' is quite another matter, and this appears to have
happened in much of the interpretation of Genesis that called
itself and is called allegorical. Here spiritualising means the
opposite, an evasion of the material meaning of the text, and
we shall use allegory here in that pejorative sense, to refer
mainly to its use in order to evade the text's reference to anything concrete and temporal.[4] It is that which above all
indicates the chief weaknesses of the ancient interpretation of
Genesis, beginning with that of Philo of Alexandria.

At this stage, we must be particularly aware that there are
dangers in the discussion of individual texts of scripture, and
perhaps none more so than those of the creation narrative. It is
surely significant that Irenaeus did not attempt to dispute the
interpretation of individual texts.[5] He refers to Genesis very
little, and rightly, for his concern is with the theology of
creation as an interpretation of the first article of the Christian
creed, itself a summary of the teaching of scripture as a whole.
Yet because certain texts have bulked large in the tradition,
and because their interpretation provides a kind of yardstick
for the theology of their user, I shall be calling attention to
them in order to show the kind of question with which we are
concerned.

1. 'In the beginning, God created the heaven and the earth.'
The first verse of Genesis is clearly crucial, though perhaps it
does not provide as significant a test as some of the later ones.
Here attention does not centre primarily on the question of
whether 'in the beginning' teaches or implies creation out of
nothing. Westermann's contention that this is not the kind of

---

[4] This must not be taken to imply that this is necessarily the case with all
allegorical interpretation. Each case must be taken on its own merits. The
contention of this paper is that much early interpretation does evade the
concrete material reference of Genesis.
[5] For example, in *Haer* 1.18.1 Irenaeus rejects gnostic allegorising, but does
not offer a counter exegesis. His concern is for a more broadly based doctrine
of creation than one derived from proof texts.

question one may appropriately ask of the writer, along with Gerhard May's convincing argument that the doctrine of creation out of nothing emerges only as the result of the church's struggle with Platonism and its extreme form, Gnosticism, suggest that one should in this case leave the question on one side.[6] Of greater theological importance is the meaning of 'heaven and earth'. Clearly intended to be a way of saying 'everything'[7] it provides, as we shall see, a field day for platonisers and allegorisers of all kinds, all those indeed who would contend that some dimensions of the created world are more real and significant than some others. Because the verse is often interpreted as teaching that the material world is in some way ontologically inferior to the 'spiritual' world, to verse 1 we should add those verses which affirm the goodness of various aspects of the creation – the earth (v. 10), the heavenly bodies (v. 18), the creatures of sea and air (v. 21), the beasts of the earth (v. 25), and, finally, after the creation of the human race, 'God saw everything that he had made, and behold, it was very good' (v. 31).

2. What is the status of the 'days'? Did the author mean a literal day? Whether or not we should accept the contention sometimes adduced, that literal days cannot be meant because there were no days until the sun and moon were created to mark them,[8] this feature of the text has always been an embarrassment for a certain kind of theologian. Embarrassment derives from two directions: the scientific or philosophical – and it is significant that many modern supposedly scientific objections to this way of speaking are the same kind as those made by ancient philosophers – and the theological. Various attempts have been made to allegorise the feature, for example that of Augustine, which we shall meet below. Like other features of Augustine's thought, this derives from a refusal to recognise the self-limitation of God in creation, the fact that he can be conceived to 'take his time'. For Augustine, creation 'must have been' instantaneous, and the days only introduced as a concession to human limitation. It is with this theologian that there comes into theology the notion of creation as the product of a kind of abstract omnipotence, inadequately related

---

[6] Gerhard May, *Creatio ex Nihilo. The Doctrine of 'Creation out of Nothing' in Early Christian Thought*, translated by A. S. Worrall (Edinburgh: T. & T. Clark, 1994).

[7] Claus Westermann, *Genesis 1–11. A Commentary*, translated by J. J. Scullion (London: SPCK, 1984), p. 101.

[8] *Luther's Works*, 1, *Lectures on Genesis chapters 1–5*, edited by J. Pelikan (St. Louis: Concordia, 1958), p. 19.

to the economy of salvation, which is precisely what provides the demonstration that in other respects, too, God allows time for his purposes to work themselves out and that therefore temporality is an indispensable feature of God's interaction with the world.

3. Another verse whose early interpretation is pregnant with menace for the future is that concerning the creation of the two lights, 'the greater light to rule the day, and the lesser light to rule the night'. It must be one of the great disasters of theological history that the lessons of this verse for the doctrine of creation were so long in the learning. Do we have here an early attempt at what can be called a kind of demythologising? There are traces of the ancient view that the sun and the moon are deities – do they not 'rule' the day and the night? – but more significant are the differences. 'What distinguishes the priestly account among the many creation stories of the Ancient Near East is that for P there can only be one creator and that all else that is or can be, can never be anything but a creature.'[9] Everywhere else in the ancient world the sun and moon – and it is significant that here they are not named, but simply described as lights – were at least semi-divine agencies, who ruled the earth, but not in the subordinate way they are here granted. They are, to use one slightly exaggerated way of putting it, 'Gods nothing! Lamps and clocks that Jahve made and hung up there.'[10] Christian theology had to come to terms with the ancient assumption of the divinity of the heavenly bodies in a somewhat more sophisticated form, that of Aristotle's teaching of the perfection, eternity – and therefore uncreatedness – of the heavenly bodies. It was what theologians made of this teaching that determined much of the character of their theologies of creation. This point becomes particularly important in the light of the history of the relation between the doctrine of creation and the rise of modern science. For if the heavenly bodies are eternal, are they truly created?

4. What is to be made of v. 27, 'So God created man in his own image . . . ; male and female he created them'? Without needing to go into the history of the interpretation of this verse, and particularly into the question of whether human sexual differences are here meant to be in some way constitutive of the image of God, we can at least say that our material constitution is in a central way important for the writer, as it

[9] Westermann, *Genesis*, p. 127.
[10] R. W. Jenson, *Story and Promise. A Brief Theology of the Gospel About Jesus* (Philadelphia: Fortress Press, 1973), p. 22.

is for the rest of the Old Testament.[11] Recent Old Testament
commentators have stressed this side of things. According to
von Rad, 'one will do well to split the physical from the spiritual
as little as possible: the whole man is created in God's image'.[12]
Qualifying this, Westermann has claimed that the stress is
less on the nature of man but on the divine action of creating a
counterpart. 'Form critical considerations ... support the
opinion ... that the creator created a creature that corresponds
to him, to whom he can speak, and who listens to him.'[13] But
this does not deny the general point that Genesis teaches close
relations between man and nature. The human creature is
created in *continuity* with the other creatures, yet is in some
way, under God, also above and responsible for them. Once
again, what is made of this in the tradition is of incalculable
importance for future theological accounts of human being,
because, as we shall see, any tendency to spiritualise the verses
tends to accentuate the discontinuity of man with nature at
the expense of the continuity. Gnosticism was an extreme
example of this tendency, but it has also marked the pages of
more orthodox theology.

II Platonism Triumphant:
Philo, Origen and Augustine

As soon as we come to Philo of Alexandria (born about 20 BC),
we find something of a pig's breakfast being made of the text of
Genesis. It is not fair to say that Philo plays fast and loose with
the text. He is an interpreter of the Bible who treats it as an
inspired writing. (Indeed, as was the case also with Origen,
that is part of the problem: a false allegorising can arise from
too desperate an attempt to find inspiration in every verse.)
Nor is it fair to accuse him of deliberately subordinating
biblical interpretation to platonising assumptions. It is clear
that Platonic assumptions do affect his interpretation of
Genesis, as they do those of every other interpreter, then and
perhaps also now. The question to be asked, however, is
whether the assumptions override essential points made by
the text, and particularly its celebration of the goodness of the
whole of the created order, material and 'spiritual' alike.

When we examine Philo's interpretation of Genesis in this
light, we meet our first problematic interpretation of Genesis

[11] See here Hans Walter Wolff, *Anthropology of the Old Testament*, translated
by Margaret Kohl (London: SCM Press, 1974).
[12] Gerhard von Rad, *Genesis. A Commentary*, translated by J. S. Marks
(London: SCM Press, 1963), p. 56.
[13] Westermann, *Genesis*, p. 157

1.1. When the latter says that God created heaven and earth, Philo understands it to refer to a two-stage creation, with God creating first the intelligible world of forms (the heavenly or intelligible world) and then the material or sensible world. 'In the beginning' according to this scheme means the ontological precedence of the incorporeal heaven over the corporeal earth. 'Wishing to make this visible world, he previously moulded the intelligible . . .'.[14] Moreover, although he affirms that 'in the beginning' involves the denial of any teaching that the world is without beginning and everlasting,[15] this falls short of what Christian theology was later to call creation out of nothing. 'Philo already knows . . . that God eternally creates the spiritual world, while the visible cosmos has a specific beginning.'[16]

The platonising interpretation of Genesis which effectively posits a hierarchy of createdness, with the lower preceded by the higher, is combined with another development which was also fateful for later history. In effect what emerged was a doctrine that while the material world was in every respect temporal, the heavenly world represented a kind of eternal creation. This undoubtedly represented a modification of Plato's views, and one which the philosopher would not have accepted, for he had held to the eternity of the forms: they could not be created, because they existed timelessly, like the truths of mathematics. The forms were for Plato external to and ontologically co-eternal with the demiurge. By being transformed by Philo into part of the created order, they are reduced in status, and are brought from outside God into the divine mind, so that Philo can speak of 'the world of the ideas that have no other place than the divine Reason'.[17] But the transfer results in a compromise which was to dog the tradition at least until the Reformation. Though the forms are created, they are eternally created, consequently to a degree sharing divine status as part of the heavenly world,[18] and thus they maintain their superiority to matter. Thus matter is implicitly, if not explicitly, demoted to a lower order of being. All may be very good, but some things are more very good than others, so that the creation is understood in dualist terms. The spiritual or rational world is created but created as eternal; while the

---

[14] Philo, *On the Account of the World's Creation given by Moses*, IV, 16.
[15] Philo, *Creation*, II, 7.
[16] Gerhard May, *Creatio ex Nihilo*, pp. 19f.
[17] Philo, *Creation*, V, 20.
[18] We realise in this respect the importance of Barth's insistence that heaven as much as earth is fully part of the created order. *Church Dogmatics* 3/1, pp. 17f.

material world is created with a temporal beginning, and therefore lower on the great chain of being.

It is to Origen that is owed an intensification of the process of the spiritualising of the creation, and much of his allegorising does not so much interpret scripture as deprive it of some of its most crucial teaching. While we are not concerned with all the details of Origen's doctrine of creation, we need to know enough to provide a background. There is, as in Philo, a tendency to conceive of a two-stage creation, with the intelligible world prior in both intention and time to the material. Moreover, the Fall is transferred to the 'time' before the creation of the material world, so that the whole of the creation story is spiritualised. In its turn, the concept of the pre-mundane Fall tends to make the material world a place of punishment, albeit punishment understood as reformative, and education. Origen is in all things a good liberal, and that means for both good and ill. Another characteristically Platonist feature of Origen's thought is the preference for unity to plurality as a desirable feature of reality. The mark of this rather platonising interpretation of the doctrine is to be found in a particular way of interpreting Genesis 1. As we shall see, there is reason to believe that much of the difference between Genesis and the Platonist tradition is to be found in the former's affirmation of that plurality which, as the Platonists rightly taught, derives from the materiality of the experienced world. What Platonism found to be a problem, indeed the occasion for, or even the cause of, evil, Genesis affirms as coming from the hand of God.

Origen shared both of Philo's central principles, the inspiration of scripture and the necessity for allegorical interpretation. Indeed, his belief in inspiration led to enormous efforts to wring inspired meaning from every verse of scripture.[19] Allegory begins in embarrassment, but also in a form of naiveté. It is a way both of being a biblical 'fundamentalist' and of playing fast and loose with the text, and it led Origen to the belief that scripture had to be interpreted in three senses, in exposition of the literal or fleshly meaning, the moral or 'psychic' and the intellectual or spiritual, the last of which was only for the τελειος or perfect in the faith. Tending to believe that the third form of exposition is the highest, Origen is like many a modern rationalist in being sceptical about the

---

[19] See here J. W. Trigg, *Origen. The Bible and Philosophy in the Third-Century Church* (Atlanta: John Knox, 1983), pp. 120–8, and particularly pp. 121f.: 'Allegory, is, like so many aspects of Origen's thought, a legacy of Greece. . . . It is the Platonists who provided, in their understanding of myth and symbol, a religiously satisfying explanation of allegory.'

historical truth of some of the verses of Genesis, for example, the 'days' of Genesis 1 and the eating of the fruit of the forbidden tree in Genesis 3. 'I do not think anyone will doubt that these are figurative expressions which indicate certain mysteries through a semblance of history and not through actual events.'[20] I do not wish to suggest that Origen is necessarily wrong about this, but would simply note that the kind of problems that have arisen in more recent times, for example over Darwinism, did not face the church with unprecedented difficulties, though it is sometimes assumed that until the nineteenth century everybody naively believed in the 'literal' truth of every verse.[21]

The problem with Origen lies not in this – after all, this paper is designed to recommend a theological approach to interpretation between 'literalism' and allegorising – so much as in what he made of his spiritualising hermeneutic. Let us look at some examples. While it is difficult always to be clear about precisely what he means, he appears to take the whole of Genesis 1 and 2, or much of it, to refer to the first stage of creation, the making of the ideal world. Genesis 1.26 refers to the creation of pre-existent intelligences, and 'male and female' refers not to sexual differentiation but to the pre-existent Christ and his bride, the church.[22] The differences from Philo emerge both in this and in the fact that the creation of heaven 'in the beginning' refers to the creation not of Platonic ideas but of the λογικα, a finite number of spiritual beings, created to spend their days (?) in contented contemplation of the deity. Indeed, Genesis 2 is understood to be also concerned not with the first man and woman but with pre-existent spirits possessing 'ethereal' rather than material bodies. As we have already seen, even the Fall is pre-historical in Origen's account. In attempting to defend the faith of the church against Gnostic charges about the unfairness of the distribution of human lots on this earth, he traces inequalities of fortune back to a pre-existent Fall in which the spiritual beings fell away from their contemplation of God.

To understand the Platonic pedigree of this reading of Genesis, it must be realised that the fall of the spirits is a fall into plurality and materiality. The second, and far inferior creation, is of the material world, which is devised as a place of training and rehabilitation for the fallen spirits. Even the skins

[20] *Princ* 3.4.1.
[21] *Princ* 4.3.1 shows that Origen had difficulties in the interpretation of the 'days' of Genesis.
[22] Henri Crouzel, *Origen*, translated by A. S. Worrall (Edinburgh: T. & T. Clark, 1989), p. 218.

with which Adam and Eve clothe themselves are brought into the allegorical picture. They represent the earthly bodies which the human race must wear until it finally makes its way back to God, which for Origen means an ascension from materiality and plurality into the pure spiritual unity which is union with God. If we think that this is allegory gone mad, we shall be right, but must remember that Gnostic theories were even wilder. How soon is there decline from the measured refusal of Irenaeus to play this kind of game at all.

Augustine's interpretation – or rather interpretations, for he worried about Genesis continually – also take us into a far more ordered world. This means that they are more dangerous, for it is easy to miss their Origenistic inheritance. Although there are continuities between Philo, Origen and Augustine, the distinctive character of the latter, especially in contrast with Origen, is that while Origen is a speculative theologian of reason, Augustine is a theologian of the will. After Athanasius' achievement in distinguishing God and the creation christologically, it was easier to rely on a distinction between the being of God and his will. This does not mean that Augustine is unwilling to rationalise; clearly, he does rationalise, just as he sometimes allegorises, albeit in a rather different way from his great predecessor. But he is far more willing to take the text literally, and there is now no more nonsense about a pre-temporal Fall. Indeed, so far as Genesis 2–3 is concerned, Augustine tends rather to literalism, and is the fountain-head of that Western doctrine of original sin that tends too much to a literal reading of the story of Adam and Eve.[23] Like Origen, Augustine would prefer that human reproduction did not take the messily material form that it does. This leads him to one of the spiritualising readings of Genesis to which we must refer. Augustine finds it difficult to believe that the instruction to 'be fruitful and multiply' in v. 28 really means what it says. It must, he says, ideally be taken of spiritual fecundity, and 'was changed into carnal fecundity only after sin'.[24]

But that is not the only problem that Augustine had with the first chapter of Genesis, which troubled him again and again. That his first attempt at a literal reading of Genesis 'remains incomplete', as his editor says, 'bears witness to Augustine's inability to offer a literal interpretation of the text'.[25] It is when he attempts a theological reading that the

[23] Especially the latter, unfortunately.
[24] Augustine, *Ad Man* 19.
[25] Roland J. Teske, 'Introduction', *St Augustine on Genesis*, *The Fathers of the Church. A New Translation*, vol. 84 (Washington: Catholic University of America Press, 1991), p. 3.

problems begin to appear, chief among them the fact that he is unable to interpret the text in the light of the economy, the biblical account of God's actions taking place in time, with the result that his understanding of divine action becomes abstract and essentially at variance with the spacious movement of the author of Genesis. If God is omnipotent will, Augustine seems to believe, he must create all things instantaneously. Here he was anticipated by Philo, who was also embarrassed by talk of the days.[26] 'The reason for [the six day creation] is that six is the number of perfection. It is not that God was constrained by the intervals of time, as if he could not have created all things simultaneously. . . . No, the reason was that completion or perfection of the works is expressed by the number six.'[27] Because God is timelessly eternal, nothing that he does can be understood to take time. That is not to deny that Augustine wrestles page after page with the meaning of 'in the beginning'. Nevertheless, the kind of questions that he asks suggests that he is unable to come to terms with an economic reading of the passage, suggesting as he does that the language of days is only there for the sake of the finite reader.[28] Once again, allegory comes to his assistance, but at the expense of the text. In *Two Books on Genesis against the Manichees*, written in AD 388 soon after his conversion, Augustine treats the days as accommodation to human weakness, seeing them first as seven ages of the world,[29] and then as stages of the spiritual life.[30]

Crucial to an understanding of Augustine's doctrine of creation, and perhaps indicative of a residual Manichaeism, is his view of a two stage creation, in which he is once again closer to Philo than to Origen. He believes that Genesis 1.1–2 teaches a creation in which there is a definite order, if not of time, then of ontology. Of the first verse, he says: 'Clearly the heaven of heavens, which you created, "in the beginning" . . . is some kind of intellectual creature.' In some way, although it is definitely created, this partakes in God's eternity. The second stage is a double one, involving first the creation of matter and

---

[26] 'For it is likely that God does all things at the same time . . .', Philo, *Creation*, III, 13.

[27] Augustine, *Civ* II. 30f.

[28] *Gen ad Litt* 3, 7.

[29] *Gen ad Litt* 23ff. In this, Augustine anticipates those allegorisers who seek to show that the six days can be made consistent with a kind of evolutionary picture.

[30] *Gen ad Litt* 25. Luther is contemptuous of Augustine's mystical interpretation of the text, as well of his and Hilary's view that God created instantaneously, *Luther's Works*, 1, *Lectures on Genesis chapters 1–5*, pp. 4–5.

then its shaping into forms in the light of the first creation.[31] It is the latter which interests Augustine, so that at times the reader wonders, as does Augustine himself, whether there is a residual Greek doctrine of the eternity of matter. He asks, 'before you fashioned that formless matter into various forms, there was nothing?' and answers that 'there was this formless matter, entirely without feature'.[32] But matter was not eternal: 'though all formed things were made from this matter, this matter itself was still made from absolutely nothing'.[33] But matter's creation out of nothing does little for its status; it is generally not of much importance, and indeed – echoes of Plotinus here[34] – scarcely in existence at all. For Augustine, the first two verses of Genesis produce a definite hierarchy of being: 'From nothing you created heaven and earth, distinct from one another; the one close to yourself, the other close to being nothing.'[35]

We cannot emphasise this too strongly. Matter is not 'very good', but 'close to being nothing'. Once again, it seems that if everything is very good, some are definitely less very good than others.[36] Once again we have evidence that the Platonic pull on Augustine is very strong, and seriously distorts his reading of the text, which it effectively contradicts or at the very least subverts. There is an interesting passage in the *Confessions*

---

[31] It is important to be aware of the fact that Augustine believes in the eternity of the forms, though it is a created eternity (if that is not a contradiction). 'The ideas are certain original and principal forms of things, i.e. reasons, fixed and unchangeable, which are not themselves formed, and being thus eternal and existing always in the same state, are contained in the Divine Intelligence. And though they themselves neither come into being nor pass away, nevertheless, everything which can come into being and pass away and everything which does come into being and pass away is said to be formed in accord with these ideas.' Augustine, *De Div Quaest* 83, 46, 2, MPL XL. 30, translation from *Saint Augustine. Eighty-Three Different Questions* by D. L. Mosher (Washington: Catholic University of America Press, 1977), p. 80. We really must take extreme exception to a theology that speaks of entities other than God which are 'stabiles atque incommutabiles . . . formatae non sunt . . . aeternae ac semper eodem sese habentes'.

[32] Augustine, *Conf* 12.3.

[33] Augustine, *Ad Man* 6, compare *Conf* 12. 8.

[34] Plotinus, *Enn*.

[35] Augustine, *Conf* 12.7.

[36] This is particularly to be seen in Augustine's preferred interpretation of the creation of light and darkness in the Genesis account. Although he confesses that this may refer to 'two divisions of the physical universe', he prefers that it describe the good and evil angels. That he is thus manifestly introducing an ontological hierarchy into his interpretation is indicated by his teaching of the eternity of the angels in *Civ* 12.16. *Civ* 12.22, 'he created man's nature as a kind of mean between angels and beasts', suggests the same drive to ontological hierarchy.

where he takes issue with those who interpret the opening
verses of Genesis in a way that may appear to us to be its
manifest meaning, of being a brief and comprehensive preliminary characterisation of the whole of the visible world. He
does not even take them seriously enough to think such
opponents worthy of engaging in argument.[37] Such, I suspect,
may also be the judgement of future generations who will not
be able to understand why we in our time are so obsessed with
reading Genesis in the light of our current preoccupation with
science.

III Platonism Modified: Basil of Caesarea

But are we asking too much of Augustine? That it is not
entirely asking the impossible of earlier theologians to suggest
that they stand a little more apart from their philosophical
assumptions is shown by the interesting case of Basil of
Caesarea. His *Hexaemeron*[38] shows many of the marks of a
platonising approach, and he was indeed criticised by Theodore
of Mopsuestia for excessive platonising.[39] He is less uncom-
promising than Irenaeus on the fundamental unity of the work
of creation, and shows signs of a dualism. Yet his tendencies
to dualism are more than compensated by other aspects of his
theological interpretation of the text. His contribution to the
doctrine of creation is best understood in the context of a
struggle with Platonism, and particularly that of his predecessor Origen. As we have seen, there are in Origen a
number of problematic features which derive partly from the
platonising interpretation of Genesis which reveals a tendency
to allegorise uncomfortable aspects of the text and a suspicion
of both the goodness and plurality or variety of the material
world. What is interesting about the work of Basil is the way
in which he struggles with, and rejects, many of these ideas,
although many of them were later to receive a fresh incarnation
in the work of Augustine.

The *Hexaemeron* of Basil is, as the name implies, a study of
the six days of creation. There is much in the work that is
dated, for it accepts a cosmology that is not indispensable to an
interpretation of Genesis and would be rejected today on

---

[37] Augustine, *Conf* 12.17–18.
[38] Basil of Caesarea, *Hexaemeron*, in *A Select Library of Nicene and Post-Nicene
    Fathers of the Christian Church*, second series vol. 8, edited by Philip Schaff
    and Henry Wace (Edinburgh: T. & T. Clark, 1989), pp. 52–107.
[39] Henry Chadwick, 'Philoponos the Christian Theologian', *Philoponos and the
    Rejection of Aristotelian Science*, edited by Richard Sorabji (London:
    Duckworth, 1987), p. 51.

scientific grounds. More significant for our purposes are the
traces of a platonising tendency in some of the things that
Basil says. It is important to make the point that, like all
theologians, he belongs to his time. Most significant in this
respect is section 5 of the first homily, in which an Origenist
meditation on what preceded the creation of the material world
intrudes incongruously on the preceding sections: 'all the
orderly arrangement of pure intelligences who are beyond the
reach of our mind . . .'. The end of that paragraph could have
come from Philo: 'after the invisible and intellectual world, the
visible world, the world of the sense began to exist'.

However, it is an intrusion in the flow of what Basil has to
say, and the signs of his distancing of himself from the
philosophy of his day are as follows. First, there is a series of
arguments against the view that the world has existed for ever.
Basil celebrates the infinity of God's creative power (I.2) and
distinguishes between different forms of creative activity: 'Not
God worked, God formed, but God created' (I.7). He goes on to
argue that if matter is uncreated, as the Greeks taught, it has
the same honour as God, while the idea of judgement implies
that the world must have an end. Those who study astronomy
discover much that is true, 'except one thing . . . They have not
known how to raise themselves to the idea of the consummation of all things . . . and to see that the world must change
if souls pass from this life to a new life' (I.4). But that the new
life is understood more after the manner of Irenaeus than of
Origen's disembodied world is suggested by the fact that
Basil has a very positive view of the material world. For him,
the visible world is not the place of *disorder*, as it was for so
many philosophers, but of a wonderful order. At the very
opening of the work we read, 'It is right that any one beginning to narrate the formation of the world should begin with
the good order which reigns in visible things.' Moreover, he is
positively enthusiastic about variety and diversity, which are
not features of the world to be escaped so much as evidence of
the richness of creation. He has an enthusiasm for the variety
of species worthy of a Darwinist. Especially in view of the
fact that the doctrine of fixed species helped to cause much of
the strife between Darwinist and Christian, it is worth pausing
to read at length Basil's disquisition on the variety of tree
life:

> What a variety in the disposition of their several parts. And
> yet, how difficult is it to find the distinctive property of each
> of them, and to grasp the difference which separates them
> from other species. Some strike deep roots, others do not;
> some shoot straight up and have only one stem, others

> appear to love the earth and, from their roots upwards, divide into several shoots . . . What variety there is in bark! Some plants have smooth bark, some have only one layer, others several. What a marvellous thing! (V.7)

And that is not all. Basil's enthusiasm for describing the wonders of the natural world nearly distracts him from his task ('But I perceive that an insatiable curiosity is drawing out my discourse beyond its limits', V.8).

Perhaps more important, in view of the fact that versions of some of the features I have mentioned were anticipated by Irenaeus, are Basil's objections to Aristotle's argument that, because their motion was circular, the heavenly bodies must be eternal. Even circular motion, he argues, requires a beginning and therefore an end (I.3). (This question, as is well known, recurs again in connection with Galileo's argument with the papal authorities. Had the latter read their Basil and Philoponos more attentively than their Aristotle, the history of the relations of science and religion might have been rather different.) There appear also other arguments against the divinity of the heavenly bodies, and attacks on astrology. The heavenly bodies do serve as signs, but it is overstepping scripture to say 'that our lives depend upon the motion of the heavenly bodies' (VI.5). The sun is, like other things, corruptible (V.1). The sheer beauty of the corruptible sun provides a measure of christological comparison. 'If the sun, subject to corruption, is so beautiful . . . what will be the beauty of the Sun of Righteousness?' (VI.2). Also of interest, in view of the later arid discussions, even until the time of Darwin and beyond, is Basil's statement about the 'days' of Genesis' account. When scripture says 'one day' it means that it wishes to establishes the world's relation to eternity, and is depicting 'distinctions between various states and modes of action' – that is to say, different ways in which God acts in and towards the world (II.8).

IV Conclusion

This excursion into the early interpretations of our seminal text has shown a number of things. One is that those who would essay a theology of creation must work in the train of a troubled history, in which things that ought to have been said were not said by many of those who are highly authoritative for the formulation of the doctrine. The second is that for this very reason, we cannot neglect the first chapters of the Bible. They are at once seminal and deeply problematic not, I believe, in themselves, but by virtue of the use to which they have been put.

But it is also important to remember that the tradition's preoccupation with Genesis has led to a serious neglect of other passages, and particularly those in the New Testament which make it clear that Christ is the mediator of creation as of redemption. It is the marginalising of christology which so marks Augustine's teaching, as any comparison of it with, for example, Athanasius' teaching on creation will make clear. The arguments of his *Discourses Against the Arians* are able to give new insights into the doctrine of creation because they are so centrally concerned with christology and the doctrine of God. The effect of this was to show that christology is essential to the doctrine of creation, to the extent that, interestingly, Athanasius reads Romans 1.20 to say that the eternal power and deity that are made known in the creation refer to the Word.[40]

It is remarkable how deep is the assumption that the Christian doctrine of creation is in some way the same thing as some version of the truth of Genesis. In one sense, it may be, as Luther's trinitarian reading of that text shows. But it also shows that the heartbeat of the doctrine of creation is as much to be found in the New Testament confessions of creation in, through, by and for Jesus Christ. It is these which transformed the teaching, and provided an essential basis for Irenaeus in particular to develop the characteristically Christian doctrine of creation out of nothing. It is therefore very important, as we approach Genesis, to remember that the Christian creed does not, and has never, held that God the Father created the world in six days, but that he created it freely, through his Son and Spirit, out of nothing. And this has the further implication that we are able to sketch the beginnings of a distinction between allegorical and theological interpretation of the text. The former, in the general tendency indicated by the historical episodes we have examined, owes enough to Platonic suspicions of matter to ensure distortions of the central thrust of the text. '[Moses'] purpose is to teach us, not about allegorical creatures and an allegorical world but about real creatures and a visible world apprehended by the senses.'[41] When that is interpreted rather in the light of God's economic involvement in and towards the material world through his Son and Spirit, the situation becomes different. This is not to deny that distortions

[40] '"His Eternal Power and Godhead" – thereby signifying the Son'. Athanasius, *Ar* 1.11.
[41] Luther, *Lectures on Genesis*, p. 5.

have not, and do not occur, by too hasty a reading of trinitarian categories into the text. It is rather to work on the (Irenaean) assumption that the God of the Old and New Testaments is the same God, so that the creator God is the one who sent his Son in the likeness of sinful flesh and raised him from death through the perfecting Spirit.

4. The End of Causality? The Reformers and their Predecessors

Colin E. Gunton

I Some Presuppositions

I begin with the articulation of some presuppositions and working assumptions, prejudices perhaps, and an attempt at some conceptual clarifications. The first is that a Christian theology of creation requires articulation through some conception of personal divine agency; that is to say, it attributes the existence of the world – a word used to refer to all that is not God – not to chance or mechanism but to some form of intentional action. I do not wish to suggest that the understanding of the attribution of personal agency to God the Creator is a straightforward matter, but rather that without such an affirmation we should be no longer in the realm of recognisably Christian doctrine. I shall return to this theme at the end of the paper.

The second working assumption is that during its history the conception of creation deriving from personal agency has suffered some contamination, not necessarily – though often in practice – to its detriment, notably by notions of emanation and causality. The former can be said to mark the thought of both Plotinus and Hegel, who is in many ways remarkably like the Neoplatonist. Moltmann is an interesting recent heir of this tradition.[1] The latter, causality, is, as scarcely needs to be said, characteristic of the Aristotelian forms of expression which still mark theology indelibly.

We shall engage with Aquinas later, but the problem is this. Causality is a polymorphic concept, with one meaning shading over into one another across a wide range. At one end of the range, it can indeed be construed in terms of personal agency, and indeed it is arguable that it was originally a personal notion. When John Zizioulas understands the Father as the

<hr/>

[1] Jürgen Moltmann, *Spirit of Life. A Universal Affirmation* (London: SCM Press, 1992).

αἰτια of the Trinity, or Adam as the cause of humanity, he clearly regards the notion as personal, archetypally so, indeed.[2] Similarly, one person can cause another person to do something in a way that does not impugn the latter's personality and freedom. At the other extreme, causality can be assimilated to logical implication, with Spinoza the clearest case. For him, to cause something is to *entail* it logically. While Spinoza's model is geometry and modern mechanism, there can be little doubt that he was given encouragement by some of his mediaeval predecessors.

It is here worth observing, parenthetically, that there is a case for saying that the critique of the notion of cause by Berkeley, anticipating as it did the work of Hume, is an attempt to retrieve an original and more personal construction. We should not, Berkeley holds, conceive causation as an inner-worldly chain of logical-type relations, because only God can cause in anything like that sense. What we call causality is not a type of logical implication, but observed regularities, regularities whose reliability derives from the fact that God causes them contingently – and so intentionally and voluntarily – to be what they are. Berkeley's attempt to restore a personal conception of causality in face of the threat of deist mechanism can be said to have failed for a number of reasons, but largely because it lacks a conception of mediation. However, that is not what interests us at this stage. What does is that Berkeley's attempt to destroy the notion that there is natural causality, autonomous and independent of divine action, and to replace it with a conception of a world in which everything is in some way caused by the personal God, does indicate where the centre of our question lies. Are things reliably the way that they are by virtue of some impersonal process, understood immanently – that is one of Berkeley's objections to Locke's substance language[3] – or by virtue of the omnipresent agency of God? The background to that question should become more evident as the paper proceeds, but it is worth noting that the dispute between Berkeley and his materialist opponents is in some sense but the re-run of an earlier development in late scholastic disputation.

The third presupposition of this paper is that, along with cause, the concept of will is equally important, because its use

---

[2] John D. Zizioulas, 'On Being a Person. Towards an Ontology of Personhood', *Persons, Divine and Human. King's College Essays in Theological Anthropology*, edited by Christoph Schwöbel and Colin E. Gunton (Edinburgh: T. & T. Clark, 1992), pp. 33–46, especially pp. 38–40.

[3] If it was Locke he was opposing. See David Berman, *George Berkeley. Idealism and the Man* (Oxford: Clarendon Press, 1994), pp. 33ff.

shapes the way in which personal agency is conceived to operate. The most explicit and detailed dogmatic statement of the doctrine of creation in the New Testament makes direct reference to the will of God. 'Thou hast created all things and by thy will (διὰ τὸ θέλημα σου) they were and were established (ἐκτίσθησαν) . . .' (Revelation 4.11). But, like the concept of cause, it too is problematic. What has been made of it in the tradition is far from straightforward, as one case will illustrate. The most relentless exponent (before Ockham, that is) of the notion of creation by the will of God is Augustine of Hippo. His achievement is crucial for the development of the doctrine of creation and, indeed, of modernity.[4] But, like all of Augustine's legacies, it is ambiguous, and its dubious features are well marked by the fact that later generations found it difficult to maintain an adequately personal conception of divine action in and towards the world. The reason is that although will is an essentially personal concept because it is personal agents who will, it is also one that easily collapses into impersonalism. This is because it can encourage the kind of conception of unmediated divine omnicausality that ultimately undermines rather than establishes the being of that which is willed. God can be conceived to will everything in such a way that the reality of the other is in some way or other imperilled – it becomes his 'creature' in the pejorative sense of that term. In this respect, willing and causing appear to have a similar logic, because under certain conditions both encourage a collapse into necessitarianism. Here the position of Plotinus is worth an allusion, in view of the fact that the essentially impersonal emanation of lower forms of being from the One appears to be the result of the One's willing of itself.

But let me illustrate the problem rather from the thought of one who can be said, for all his greatness, to have introduced disturbingly determinist elements into his own Reformed heritage. Jonathan Edwards appears to understand the concept of cause as an analogical one. *Created* causality is not determinist or necessitarian. 'Cause is that, after or upon the existence of which, or the existence of it after such a manner,

---

[4] See here Michael B. Foster, *The Political Philosophies of Plato and Hegel* (Oxford: Clarendon Press, 1935). 'The failure of Greek ethics to achieve a notion of will was a necessary consequence of Greek metaphysics . . .' (p. 131). The converse is that it comes from Christian revelation, and specifically in connection with its doctrine of creation. For example: 'the doctrine of Creation is the source from which the conception of sovereignty is derived. This doctrine is the fundamental doctrine of the Christian revelation . . .' (pp. 191f.).

the existence of another thing follows.'[5] But the causality exercised by God does appear to be understood in a determinist or even necessitarian manner. Along with Berkeley, Edwards wished to replace the theory that sensations were caused by substance with one that they were caused directly by God:

> The reason why it is so exceedingly natural to men to suppose that there is some latent substance, or something that is altogether hid, that upholds the properties of bodies, is because all see at first sight that the properties of bodies are such as need some cause that shall every moment have influence to their continuance, as well as a cause of their first existence. All therefore agree that there is something that is there, and upholds these properties; and it is most true, there undoubtedly is. But men are wont to content themselves in saying that it is something; but that 'something' is he by whom all things consist.[6]

This led Edwards to what a recent commentator has called his doctrine of omnicausality.[7] Michael Jinkins says that 'he wanted to demonstrate that it is reasonable to enlightened people, not only to believe that all things are causally determined, but that all things are causally determined – *by God*'. And he notes the reason: there is otherwise no way of ascending by a chain of causation to prove the existence of God.[8]

The point of all this is that neither the concept of God as cause nor the attribution of creation to his will prevents theology from lapsing into conceptions of impersonal determinism. The reasons for the fact that it has often so lapsed, and the approach to some kind of a solution, will be sought in the theological history of the West. The general contention will be that if either of those concepts are to be used, their use must be controlled by the context in which they are deployed. In the next section, we shall review, fairly summarily, some of the features of the reigning theology of creation in the Middle Ages.

---

[5] Jonathan Edwards, *Scientific and Philosophical Writings*, The Works of *Jonathan Edwards*, vol. 6, edited by Wallace E. Anderson (New Haven and London: Yale University Press, 1980), p. 350.

[6] Edwards, p. 380, cf. p. 339: 'Our perceptions, or ideas that we passively receive by our bodies, are communicated to us immediately by God while our minds are united with our bodies.'

[7] Michael Jinkins, '"The Being of Beings". Jonathan Edwards' Understanding of God as Reflected in his Final Treatises', *Scottish Journal of Theology* 46 (1993), 161–90 (164).

[8] Jinkins, pp. 172f. citing *The Freedom of the Will*, The Works of Jonathan *Edwards*, vol. 1, edited by Paul Ramsey (New Haven and London: Yale University Press, 1957), p. 182.

II Some Mediaeval Theologies of Creation

The thesis to be argued in this section is that, despite the immense differences between Aquinas and those, like Ockham, who undermined his Aristotelian conception of causality, they remain in certain crucial respects the same in their understanding of the relation of God to the world. What they have in common is reliance on the concept of cause *along with* the almost total absence from their conceptions of the mediation of creation of any trinitarian reference. It is this that makes the achievement of the Reformers, despite all the limitations that we shall observe, so remarkable. It is worth saying here, in anticipation of the outcome of the argument, that the point about trinitarian reference is that it allows a concept of the mediation of the created order that is personal and so does not abolish the space in which the creation can be properly itself.

If we begin with Aquinas, we must emphasise that it is not the case that either personal or trinitarianly conceived agency in creation is completely lacking from his thought; he is in the tradition of Augustine in teaching that creation is the outcome of the free, personal willing of the Creator. The problem is that the act of willing is rather monistically conceived. The Trinity plays little or no constitutive part in his treatment of the divine realisation of creation, as is evident already in the Question that sets the scene for his treatment of creation, number 44 of the first part of the *Summa Theologiae*: 'the first cause of things'. This question precedes the discussion of creation, which is thus introduced with a chiefly abstract and merely 'monotheistic' treatment of the status of God as first cause.[9] When we come to Question 45, 'Creation', article 7 is reached before there is mention of the trinitarian attributions, and there the distinctive forms of agency in creation are minimised rather than taken fully seriously. What emerges is a fairly strong conception of divine omnicausality.

Among the disturbing symptoms of the discussion is the rejection of Peter Lombard's view that power to create can be delegated to a creature which works *ministerially*, in apparent neglect of the pattern displayed in Genesis 1, where God does precisely that – 'Let the earth bring forth'.[10] There are other

---

[9] I am here operating with one recent and pejorative use of the word 'monotheism'. See here Christoph Schwöbel, 'Monotheismus IV. Systematisch-theologisch', *Theologische Realenzyklopädie* XXIII, 1/2, 256–62, for a demonstration of the variety of usage.

[10] Aquinas, *Summa Theologiae* I.45.5. See Francis Watson, *Text, Church and World. Biblical Interpretation in Theological Perspective* (Edinburgh: T. & T. Clark, 1994), p. 142, for the conception of mediated creation to be found in Genesis 1.

problematic features, crucial among them two which threaten
to undermine the distinct reality of the creature. First is a
denial that God acts to achieve a purpose in creating – 'he
intends only to communicate his own completeness';[11] and
second is a denial that creation puts a reality into a creature
except as a relation ('[Creation] in God is not a real relation,
but only conceptual').[12] Both of these detract from the creature's
value as creature, for they tie the creature too closely to God,
and so fail to give it space to be. We might say that they detract
from the proper substantiality of the creature. Here it should
be noted that there are two requirements for a satisfactory
construal of the relation of God and the world: adequate conceptions of the continuing relatedness of the world to God and
of that world's due reality – we might say due autonomy – in
its relation to God. It is not that Aquinas does nothing to ensure
the reality of the creature; it is rather that the *contingence* of
the creature on God (its dependence) is given more adequate
weighting than its *contingency*: its freedom to be itself. 'The
whole of what is genuinely real and true virtually exists in God
though not in creation.'[13] A similar, and stronger, point could
be made against Schleiermacher.

Many of the same ways of putting things reappear in the
thought of Duns Scotus, although there are one or two features
that might be considered to suggest significant differences.
First, the concept of cause is less prominent; and second some
reference is made to the subordinate authority of Jesus Christ
in creation, with allusion to the dialectic in John 5 of Jesus'
being able to do nothing of himself, but doing what the Father
has given him to do.[14] By contrast, Thomas virtually never
appeals to New Testament creation texts, nearly always to the
first verse of Genesis alone. His Word tends to mean the Logos
asarkos, not the incarnate Jesus Christ.[15] The point of all this

[11] Aquinas, *Summa*, 44.4.
[12] Aquinas, *Summa*, 45.3 ad 1.
[13] '. . . virtualiter in Deo, sed non totum existit in rebus creatis'. Aquinas,
Summa, I.19.6. Much difference would be made by saying: 'really exists in
the Son'. For Thomas' tendency to necessitarianism, see a sentence in the
same question: 'An effect cannot possibly escape the order of the universal
cause.'
[14] John Duns Scotus, *God and Creatures. The Quodlibetal Questions*, 8.1.17,
translated by F. Alluntis and A. B. Wolter (Washington: Catholic University
of America Press), p. 211.
[15] There is little or nothing in Thomas' text here to provide support for the
editor's assertion that 'St. Thomas' doctrine of creation is christocentric
and scriptural . . . that God created in Wisdom and the "word". This does
not appear in the foreground of most of the discussions . . . The weight
St. Thomas attached to a topic cannot be judged by the number of words
he devoted to it . . . In the present case, unless the doctrine of *Colossians* 1,

is not simply to assert the impropriety of all doctrines of the pre-incarnate Word, but to make the point that much of Western theology has been able to operate with a highly abstract theology of the second person of the Trinity, with the result that the New Testament linking of Jesus Christ and creation ceases to be determinative for the theology of creation.

When we come to the thought of William of Ockham, there are both similarities and differences. So far as the differences are concerned, Ockham is far more interested than Aquinas in the doctrine of creation out of nothing and the distinctive conception of contingency it generates, one very much derived from a stress on the free willing of the Creator. It is thus a conception of contingency *from above* rather than one from below of the kind Aquinas, and, as we have seen, Edwards, use as the basis for an argument for the existence of a first cause. We might say that Ockham's scepticism about the latter has enabled him to move to a stress on creation as an act of free and personal divine willing. Ockham is celebrated, in works on the history of science, as one who, by stressing the contingency of creation, helped to lay the ground for that celebration of the distinct reality of the world which did so much to further the advance of modern science.[16] The outcome is that, in this case, will has come to predominate over cause, so that causality's tendency to suggest logical links between God and the world is replaced by one suggesting freely willed personal creation.[17] As Oberman comments in connection with Biel's similar epistemology, a demonstration of the deficiencies of the natural knowledge of God enables an elimination of Anselmian necessity, without losing the faith seeking under-

---

15–23 is seen as central to his thought, he is no more than a religious philosopher who is the peer of Avicenna and Maimonides.' St. Thomas Aquinas, *Summa Theologiae*, vol. 8 (London: Blackfriars/Eyre and Spottiswoode, 1967), editorial note, pp. 87f.

[16] Harold Nebelsick, *The Renaissance, the Reformation and the Rise of Science* (Edinburgh: T. & T. Clark, 1992), pp. 52–63, and referring to such classics of the history of science as A. C. Crombie, *Augustine to Galileo* (London: Heinemann, 1959), vol. 2, pp. 43–5 and 79. For Ockham's conception of the contingency of the divine act of creation, see, for example, William of Ockham, *In Librum Sententiarum* LI. D17. Q1, *Opera Philosophica et Theologica* (New York: St. Bonaventure University, 1981), *Opera Theologica*, vol. III, pp. 453f.: 'quidquid Deus contingenter creat, potest contingenter illud adnilihare quandocumque placet sibi'. That is voluntarism at its most stark.

[17] Indeed, Ockham's is, as is often enough noted, a highly voluntarist conception of deity, and he holds against Scotus that the divine essence cannot be distinguished from the divine will; 'essentia divina nullo modo distinguiter a voluntate divina sed omni modo identitatis quo essentia est eadem essentiae etiam essentia est eadem voluntati'. *Opera Theologica*, vol. IV, p. 663.

standing.[18] What this enables Ockham to do is to establish, in some contrast to Aquinas, a central place for the doctrine of creation out of nothing.[19]

But, and here the similarities between the two mediaevals present themselves to view, the matter is not so straight-forward. I return to the point that certain concepts of will are as problematic as certain concepts of cause. The other desideratum for a doctrine of creation, a satisfactory conception of the continuing relation of Creator God to created world, remains lacking. There is contingency, but little account of the stability which derives from a continuing dependence of the world upon God. This is a theme which will recur, but for now the point to make is that Ockham continues to couch his discussion in terms of causality, rather monistically conceived, and so is unable to prevent the emergence of a conception of divine omnicausality, whose final outcome is an inadequate conception of creaturely reality. In that respect, the significant feature of Ockham's discussion of creation is not so much – as is often supposed to be the problem – the introduction of a radical doctrine of *potentia absoluta* as the entirely non-trinitarian treatment of creation, perhaps best exemplified in the fact that he can refer to the opening verses of the Gospel of John without noting the part played in its conception of creation by the mediation of the Word.[20]

As we know well, to Ockham goes the credit – if one believes in the legitimacy of modernity – of so cutting off the world from its Creator that God eventually disappears from the picture altogether. That is the other, opposite but equal, side of the doctrine of omnicausality. Might things have been otherwise if certain of the things said by the Reformers in this context had been more clearly heard? While one should probably not speculate about the hypotheticals of history, it remains the case that Luther and Calvin have things to say that are quite remarkable in their historical context – one could almost use that much abused word revolutionary – even though with them too a certain ambivalence remains.

[18] H. Oberman, *The Harvest of Medieval Theology* (Cambridge, Mass: Harvard University Press, 1963), pp. 40f.
[19] 'Creatio est simpliciter de nihilo, ita quod nihil extrinsecum et essentiale rei praedicat; similiter in adnihilatione nihil remanet; igitur si aliquid essentiale rei creabili et adnihilabili praecedat et remanet non adnihilabitur nec creabitur.' Ockham, *In Librum Sententiarum* LI. D2. Q4, *Opera Theologica*, vol. II, p. 116.
[20] *Quodlibetal Questions* 2, Q4. Art. 2. Ockham understands John 1.3 to mean that God made all other things through himself (omnia alia a Deo per ipsum facta sunt), *Opera Theologica*, vol. 9, p. 215.

III Luther and Calvin

In view of what we have just noted about the non-trinitarian
treatment of creation in the Middle Ages, Luther's claim that
he was the only person to have understood the first chapter of
Genesis is only slightly exaggerated. The change he brings
about is remarkable. Unlike Augustine – of whom it can be
said, without much exaggeration, that he was more interested
in allegorising the text in the interests of his view that God
created all things instantaneously and reading between the
lines a Platonic two-order creation – Luther interprets it in
trinitarian fashion.[21] It is now fashionable, and perhaps
justifiable, to reject as fanciful the traditional interpretation of
the 'Let us' in Genesis as referring to a plurality, and therefore
a three. What is of interest, in any case, is not the plural so
much as the manifoldness of the concept of mediation to be
found in the passage, as Francis Watson has shown.[22] Luther
is right to read it in the way that he does, especially in the light
of a theological understanding of the unity of the Testaments.
Both witness the action of the same God, and if he is indeed
triune, then his Old Testament revelation should also be so
understood. 'Luther', says Regin Prenter, 'always speaks of
creation in terms of the Trinity.'[23]

Of importance here is what this trinitarian reading enables
Luther to say. First, he denies Augustine's neoplatonising view
that matter is almost nothing ('I disagree entirely'). To the
contrary, the text teaches us 'not about mystical days of knowledge among angels and an allegorical world, but about real
creatures and a visible world apprehended by the senses'.
Second, recognising the concepts of mediation in the chapter,
Luther reaffirms that which was scarcely of interest to
Aquinas, that God created heaven and earth out of nothing. He
can do this because he sees it to take place through the work of
the Son, who adorns and separates the crude mass which was
brought out of nothing; and the Spirit, who makes alive.[24]
(How, he asks, could the word rendered spirit in Genesis 1.2
refer to the wind when the wind did not then exist?) Whatever
we are to make of his exegesis, the fact remains that with
Luther doctrines to which little more than lip service had been

[21] *Luther's Works*, 1, *Lectures on Genesis chapters 1–5*, edited by J. Pelikan (St.
Louis: Concordia, 1958), p. 9. Luther is contemptuous of Augustine's mystical
interpretation of the text, as well of his and Hilary's view that God created
instantaneously, pp. 4–5.
[22] Watson, *Text, Church and World*, pp. 140–4.
[23] Regin Prenter, *Spiritus Creator. Luther's Concept of the Holy Spirit*
(Philadelphia: Muhlenberg, 1953), pp. 192f.
[24] Luther, *Lectures on Genesis*, p. 9.

paid for centuries come again to life. The result is that Luther's
theology of creation is one not of absolute so much as of
personal dependence: its atmosphere is of grace and gratitude.
'For here we may see how the Father has given Himself to
us, with all that he has created, and how abundantly he has
cared for us in this life . . .'.[25] There are, of course, problems,
and it might be said that here too more might have been
done for the substantiality of the created world. There is to
be seen in Luther's treatment of creation in the *Greater
Catechism*[26] a tendency to the reduction of the created world to
its instrumental use for us, something which was taken further
by Schleiermacher.

Calvin's legacy is similar, and again somewhat ambiguous.
As is well known, his theology of creation has an existential
orientation similar to Luther's, articulated as it is in a
dialectic of the knowledge of God the Creator and of the
knowledge of ourselves. The characteristic Reformation
polemic against scholastic abstraction can be observed in his
claim that these two together constitute the sum of wisdom.
There is no interest in abstract speculation. But the other
side is also apparent, in Calvin's tendency to narrow the
scope of a theology of creation to its anthropological relevance,
a narrowing similar to Luther's. Although he affirms the
doctrine of creation out of nothing in his commentary on
Genesis,[27] there is surprisingly little interest in it in the
Institutes. There is, again in line with Luther, a new interest
in the christological mediation of creation. Yet what interests
Calvin is not speculation, Augustinian or other, about
creation out of nothing, so much as the relevance of conceptions
of divine action for the confidence of the believer in God's
government of things.

It should not be denied that some of the implications of
creation out of nothing do appear in Calvin's thought, and are
of crucial importance in that process of freeing the created

---

[25] Luther, *Lectures on Genesis*, p. 98.
[26] *Greater Catechism*, p. 98. Luther's exposition of the creed in the second part
of *The Greater Catechism* appropriates creation to God the Father, following
the rather modalistic manner of the Apostles' Creed. He also understands
creation personally, from the point of view of the believer. Creation means
that: 'I understand and believe that I am God's creature, that is, He gave me
and preserves for me continually my body, my soul and life, etc.' Luther is
not very interested in the non-personal world for its own sake. Creatures are
there to 'serve for my use and the necessities of life' (p. 97). But there is no
trace of the causal conception of creation which, as we shall see, is so
dominant in the thought of his predecessors.
[27] John Calvin, *Genesis*, translated by John King (Edinburgh: Banner of Truth,
1965), p. 70.

order from the Platonic and Aristotelian intermediate quasi-agencies so essential for the development both of a satisfactory doctrine of creation and of modern science. The presentation of the created order as a semiotic system, a system of signs which as a system pointed beyond itself to its maker, helped to assure the relative independence of creation from the Creator without which a proper notion of contingency could not develop. But there is an Achilles' heel, which can be inspected through a study of Calvin's writings on the continuing relation of Creator with his creation. His real interaction with his predecessors comes in the extended treatment of providence that dominates the later chapters of Book I of the *Institutes*.

In it we meet a theology of the omnipotent will of God containing more than a few echoes of the merely monotheistic treatment which we met in the Schoolmen. Augustine is cited in support of the claim that there is no higher cause of things than God's will.[28] Repeatedly it is asserted that there is no such thing as chance. What may appear to be chance faith recognises as a secret impulse from God.[29] In what may be a criticism of a Thomist conception, Calvin refuses to say 'that God is the first agent because he is the beginning and cause of all motion'. Quite the reverse: 'believers comfort themselves with the solace that they suffer nothing except by God's ordinance and command . . .'.[30] '[P]rovidence is lodged in the act', not simply in the foreknowledge of God. Elsewhere he appeals to Augustine in defence of a belief that 'nothing is more absurd than that anything should happen without God's ordaining it, because it would then happen without any cause'.[31] What are we to make of all this? There are three main points.

1. It is sometimes remarked that Calvin is not very interested in the third possible form of knowledge, that of the world in and for itself, though much is made in treatments of his relation to science of the encouragement given to the development of science by his celebration of the glory of God visible in the created world. But the question must remain whether the sum of wisdom includes knowledge of the world also. It has been argued, by T. F. Torrance[32] and Harold Nebelsick in particular, that it was the recovery of the doctrine of creation out of nothing that facilitated the emergence of the belief, so

[28] John Calvin, *Institutes*, I. 14. 1.
[29] Calvin, *Institutes*, I. 16. 2 and 9.
[30] Calvin, *Institutes*, I. 16. 3.
[31] Calvin, *Institutes*, I. 16. 8.
[32] Thomas F. Torrance, *Divine and Contingent Order* (Oxford: Oxford University Press, 1981).

important for the development of modern science, in the contingency of the world. Certainly Calvin's world is contingent in the sense that it does not have to be, because it is freely created by the will of a personal God. But it is not so securely contingent in the sense that what happens in it does not have to happen as it does. Contingency has, it must be remembered, two senses, referring (1) to the dependence of the world on God, a sense that was undoubtedly present in Aquinas; and also (2) to the world's non-necessity, particularly in relation to its divine source. Calvin in fact, rightly careful as he is to escape any entanglement in the concepts of fortune or chance, appears also, as we have seen, to deny any concept of contingency. On the one hand, he denies a Stoic necessitarianism, but on the other by appearing to equate the concepts of contingency and chance, has rightly or wrongly laid himself open to the same charge. The assertion of divine willing alone is not adequate to escape a tendency to necessitarianism.[33]

2. The immense and rather repetitive length at which Calvin wrestles with the problem of divine agency in relation to the world no doubt has something to do with what Bouwsma has called his anxiety.[34] These were times very much imbued with a sense of Heraclitean flux and the uncertainty of things, as that historian also records. But there are also signs that Calvin was somewhere himself uneasy about the apparently determinist direction of his thought, as his brief appeals to the concept of secondary causation reveal. He does not, however, rule out secondary causes 'in their proper place'.[35] Of the status of these secondary causes nothing is said.[36] In general therefore

---

[33] Calvin, I. 16. 8. After the equation of the two concepts of chance and contingency, the latter disappears from the discussion.

[34] William J. Bouwsma, *John Calvin. A Sixteenth Century Portrait* (New York and Oxford: Oxford University Press, 1989).

[35] Calvin, *Institutes*, I. 17. 6 and 9.

[36] It is surely significant that the concept of secondary causality was introduced in order to establish some form of limited autonomy in the creature. But it is problematic. Without a satisfactory concept of mediation, it simply replicates the problems we have met. The question that must be asked is whether the concept of secondary causation is an attempt to ensure the relative autonomy of the creature in the absence of an adequate conception of the mediation of creation and of providence or conservation. Creation trinitarianly conceived is thus the necessary condition of the doctrine of creation out of nothing, because without it matter, or some other feature of the universe, becomes the mediator, *and thus eternal*. Secondary causation is therefore either too strong – producing the redundancy of God observed by Blumenberg in Ockham, and later in Deism – or it is too weak, and the world becomes once again the determined product of divine monocausality, as for example in Spinoza. Here it is instructive to return to the case of Bishop Berkeley. Berkeley rejected the concept of mediation by created substance on various

Calvin is able to give a more satisfying account of the universal providential care of God than of the correlative thesis that human agents are responsible for their actions. The reason for this is to be found in:

3. In some contrast to the rest of his theology, there is in Calvin's account of the relation of God and the world little substantive part played by Christ and the Holy Spirit. There is in the passages we have reviewed from Calvin only one statement of the christological mediation of divine action in creation.[37] Similarly, the splendid characterisation of the Spirit's universal and life-giving work – 'everywhere diffused' he 'sustains all things, causes them to grow, and quickens them in heaven and earth'[38] – is to be found in the chapter on the doctrine of the Trinity, and does not recur with the same weight in the long treatment of providence. It is at least arguable that the wholesale return to the category of cause in the theology of Edwards has something to do with the intimations of omnicausality in Calvin. And part of the reason is that we meet here somewhat more of a theology of will than of love, more of an omnipotent monocausal God than of the one who works through his two hands, the Son and the Spirit.

In concluding this section, however, my concern is to summarise the positive developments in both Luther and Calvin. There is in both of these theologians a major shift away from the language of causality to one of personal action. The achievement is that the doctrine of creation is taken out of the largely philosophical context in which it had tended to be located, where it had become a semi-independent propaedeutic for faith, and returned to the confessed creed. This is the clear outcome equally of Luther's trinitarian reading of Genesis – as well as his close relating of creation with the believer's trust in God – and of Calvin's concern with God's personal and providential oversight of the creation.[39] Thus there is much to be said for the claim that the Reformers contributed to, indeed,

---

grounds, among them that substance was unknowable and that it effectively replaced God as the real agent of creation. But his solution, lacking a trinitarian concept of mediation, failed to achieve its end.

[37] See Calvin, *Institutes*, I. 16. 4.

[38] Calvin, *Institutes*, I. 13. 14.

[39] It is perhaps worth mentioning at this stage that a link between christology and the abandonment of the scholastic idiom of causality has been observed by Ralph Del Colle to take place in some recent Roman Catholic theology. Ralph Del Colle, *Christ and the Spirit. Spirit-Christology in Trinitarian Perspective* (New York and Oxford: Oxford University Press, 1994), *passim*, though see, for example, p. 132.

achieved with little assistance from their Western predecessors, the recovery of the doctrine of creation. The heart of this achievement was (1) that in continuity with Ockham, they did much to re-establish a doctrine of the contingency of the created order on a freely willed act of God, and in this way encouraged the reappropriation of the ontological distinction of Creator from creation which had been obscured by doctrines of quasi-eternal forms and hierarchies of causes. There are on this account only two realities, Creator and creation. The significance of this is to be found in the reappropriation of the doctrine of the homogeneity of the created order. By this is meant not that there is no diversity and variety in the creation,[40] but that everything created has the same ontological status, so that, for example, it cannot be taught that the heavenly bodies consist of some ethereal or eternal substance different from that of the earth. Basil of Caesarea and others had long ago made that discovery on the grounds of the doctrine of creation.[41] Galileo's famous observation of the heavens through a telescope was a crucial step in the process of establishing that the heavenly bodies are of the same kind of material as the earth, but he was not as original as is sometimes suggested in secularising accounts of the origin of science. Equally important, (2), the Reformers began a process of replacing a conception of causality, relatively impersonally conceived, or, if not, of creation rather monistically construed in terms of will, with conceptions of agency in terms of trinitarian mediation, and that means agency far more personally conceived. Here they went far beyond their mediaeval predecessors. It follows that the God who creates the world is distinguished from all causes and emanations by the personal and intentional freedom by which he works. In that sense, the doctrine of creation represents the end of causality by virtue of its replacement by a doctrine of creation by personal agency.

IV The Problem of Mediation

The problem left behind by the Reformers, however, derives from the fact that they were less successful in developing an account of the world's continuing relation with God the Creator. What was lacking was a satisfactory conception of

[40] The abolition of the mediating function of the Platonic forms means that there can be a re-establishing of the diversity of things, in their own right, because the focus of attention is turned away from the eternal world to this one. 'God saw *everything* that he had made, and behold, it was very good.'
[41] Basil, *Hexaemeron*, i. 3; v. 1; vi. 5.

mediation, by which is intended, as will by now be evident, a trinitarian one. Tradition, as in the Apostles' Creed, and even in the confessions of the rule of faith that are quoted by Irenaeus, attributes creation to the Father, salvation to the Son and life in the church (etc.) to the Spirit. Dogmatically, that not only encourages modalism, but also draws attention away from the New Testament affirmations of the place of Jesus Christ in the mediation of creation as well as of salvation. That is perhaps the reason why the doctrine of creation is so often merely monotheistically, perhaps better unitarianly, construed. Rather, it should be said that creation, reconciliation and redemption are all to be attributed to the Father, all realised through the work of his two hands, the Son and the Spirit, who are, of course, themselves substantially God. There is mediation, but it is through God, not ontological intermediates. This tends to be lost when any other mediator conceived independently of the 'two hands' – Platonic forms, Aristotelian causes, Lockean or Newtonian substance – becomes the central focus of attention. Accordingly, although there is a danger of abstraction in so doing, I shall take first the christological dimensions and then the pneumatological, using as a starting point in each case some remarks of Robert Jenson.

In the first, he argues that the Cappadocian rearrangement of Origen's way of understanding the hypostases – 'making the hypostases' mutual relations structures of the one God's life rather than risers of the steps from God down to us' – cleared away the realm of intermediate beings between God and the world:

> The Trinity as such is now understood to be the Creator, over against the creature, and the three in God and their relations become the evangelical history's reality on the Creator-side of the great biblical Creator/creature divide. Across the Creator/creature distinction no mediator is needed. [Or alternatively, the incarnation is the mediation, not the logos as such.][42]

The final sentence, placed in parentheses because it is a footnote in Jenson's book, makes the essential point. The incarnation – the act of free divine interrelation with the created world – provides the model of mediation that we need. Christology, not the ontologically intermediate being represented by some (Origenistic) conceptions of the Logos, but the Son of God in free personal relation to the world,

---

[42] Robert Jenson, *The Triune Identity. God According to the Gospel* (Philadelphia: Fortress Press, 1982), pp. 106f.

indeed identification with part of that world, is the basis for
an understanding of God the Father's relations with his
creation.

Before the Cappadocians, Athanasius had already seen the
point of this in his argument that Jesus Christ is himself the
creating Word, incarnate in human flesh to complete the work
of creation. To be sure, this expresses a causal relation in the
sense that it brings something about, in particular the
reordering of relations between Creator and creation. But it
suggests a very different conception of the relation of God and
the world from that found in the work of the earlier Schoolmen. It is not mediation through immanent patterns of
causality because, as Irenaeus pointed out in opposition to the
intermediate beings of the Gnostics, God's action through the
Son is action by God in person. The reappropriation of that
position begun by the Reformers in their trinitarian reading of
the Old Testament can be taken seriously because the
incarnation demonstrates the utterly free relatedness of God
to that which he has made, and so provides an instance and
paradigm of a form of *mediated* action that requires no *intermediaries*.

The methodological point that God's action in the incarnation founds a way of understanding divine action in general
can be supplemented by the drawing out of its ontological
implication: that the stability and reliability of the world in
general does not depend on some intermediate being or beings
– the point of Berkeley's polemic against the concept of substance – but directly on God.[43] Such a suggestion of divine
omnicausality, however, can be saved from the nearly pan-
theistic implications that appear to follow from Berkeley's and

[43] Thus in early modern philosophy, 'substance' performs the same function as
the hidden essences and other scholastic beings that modern thought
believed itself to have exorcised. Michael J. McLymond, 'God the Measure:
Towards an understanding of Jonathan Edwards' Theocentric Metaphysics',
Scottish Journal of Theology 47 (1994), 43–59 shows that Edwards knew the
way that the wind was blowing. He notes (p. 53) that Edwards' idealism was
a reaction to mechanistic and materialistic world-views, especially that of
Hobbes. Edwards' view: 'there is no such thing as mechanism, if that word is
taken to be that whereby bodies act upon each other, purely and properly by
themselves' (*Scientific and Philosophical Writings*, p. 216) is glossed by
Jenson's comment. 'Edwards' critique of mechanism is an encompassing
piece of demythologizing: there are no little self-sufficient agencies besides
God, natural entities are not godlets, and therefore the world harmony is
not self-contained.' Robert Jenson, *America's Theologian. A Recommendation
of Jonathan Edwards* (New York: Oxford University Press, 1988) p. 25.
Edwards is thus understood to be seeking to secure the world for divine
involvement in opposition to the eighteenth-century notion of a self-
contained universe.

Edwards' view that everything comes directly from God. The divine causality must be understood not only as direct, but also as mediated. Edwards' statement, cited above, that 'that "something" is he by whom all things consist' should, but in his case apparently does not, take us to the eternal Son and wisdom of God. To be adequately construed, this mediated upholding, albeit without intermediaries or intermediate being(s), must be understood christologically, so that we should also take quite seriously the implications of the New Testament belief that creation coheres in Christ, or exists through him. It is stable and reliable because it is upheld in being by Christ, through whom the creation has its being. By means of a christological account of mediation, then, we are able to give some account of the stability of the creation which avoids the difficulties of both scholastic and early modern accounts.

But that supplies only one of two desiderata. The other is that some space be given to the created order, that is to say, some account of its distinctive being as creation, as other than but not apart from God – what could be called its autonomy, its ability to be itself, according to the law of its own particular being. We can make a beginning of this christologically. Let us take the humanity of Jesus as a test case, for it enables us to ask the question how this particular part of the created order is maintained in its integrity while yet being dependent on God's agency. If we ask how it is that the humanity of Jesus of Nazareth is maintained in its autonomy, the answer is in part pneumatological. If Jesus' humanity was in no way imperilled by its being that of the Word, that is because of the action of God the Spirit. The Spirit is the one who mediates the action of God the Father in such a way that the life of the Son, while deriving from the Father and dependent upon him, is given space to remain authentically human.

An account of the proper autonomy of the world must run in parallel with this, but we shall preface that by indicating something of the inadequacy of traditional accounts. That is highlighted by a second remark of Robert Jenson, this time on the conception of the work of the Holy Spirit that has dominated Western theological history. According to him, Augustine's rendering of the three persons of the Trinity functionally indistinguishable left the Western church with a highly problematic account of the causal[44] relations of God and the world. 'Augustine was left with the standard position of Western culture-religion: on the one hand there is God,

---

[44] Thus does our central problem recur in yet another place.

conceived as a supernatural entity who acts causally on us; and on the other hand there are the results among us of this causality.'[45] The resulting displacement, by what are effectively semi-mechanical conceptions of grace, of free personal action by the Spirit has had numerous deleterious effects in theology, and it can be argued that among them are the various conceptions of divine omnicausality that have distorted understandings of divine action in the world. Let us therefore look briefly at what might derive from renewed attention to pneumatology.

The resurrection of Jesus from the dead has been traditionally attributed to the Holy Spirit, and I will take it as a working hypothesis that this is an illuminating basis for consideration of action by the Spirit. The transformation of the corpse of Jesus into the conditions of the world to come is an instance of causally efficacious, but freely willed personal divine action. It has a number of features, however, which make it more satisfactory than either patterns of causality operating immanently, as in the Thomist account, or the rather monocausal accounts of Ockham, Calvin and their successors. First, it leaves room for an otherness, a space, between that which causes and that which is caused. Action by the Spirit is in no way assimilable to models of logical implication (see John 3 and Ezekiel 37), but is free, unpredictable and efficacious. It respects the reality of the other by enabling it to be that which it was created to be, in a free act of divine transformation rather than the exercise of causal power. But, second, it does not run the risk of Ockhamist arbitrariness or the mere exercise of *potentia absoluta*. The resurrection of Jesus represents the consistency of the divine action, and in a number of respects: consistency with the outcome of Jesus' obedience, as its affirmation and completion; and with the divine purposes for the creation, whose recapitulation and perfection are inaugurated in the ministry of Jesus.

Crucial here is the eschatological action of the Spirit, his enabling of created things to become what they are by anticipating what they shall be, a function inaugurated and instantiated by the resurrection of Jesus from the dead. Having said that, however, we must remember that there is eschatology and eschatology. On the one hand, there is that, whose father is perhaps Origen of Alexandria and whose greatest exponent is perhaps Augustine, which sees the end of

---

[45] Robert W. Jenson, 'The Holy Spirit', *Christian Dogmatics*, edited by C. E. Braaten and R. W. Jenson (Philadelphia: Fortress Press, 1984), vol. 2, pp. 126f.

creation as a return to the perfection of its beginning. This tends to be associated with, if it is not actually the outcome of, a Neoplatonic and emanationist view of things, according to which it is the destiny of creation to be, so to speak, rolled back into the being of God.[46] The inadequacy of this is shown by the consideration that if creation is God's self-communication, his word, then its destiny is to return to him void, for it does not become, in its own right, anything more than it once was. It simply returns whence it came as what it once was: nothing. That is to say, it has no truly eschatological teleology. On the other hand, if the Spirit is indeed the perfecting cause of creation,[47] whose function is to bring the world through Christ to a completeness which it did not have in the beginning, there is rather more to be said. The destiny of things on this account is to be presented before the throne in their perfection, not without the human creation, indeed, but transformed in such a way that their true otherness is not only respected but achieved. This is the work of the Lord who is the Spirit.

In sum, we conclude that the Reformers and their pre-decessors have enabled us to move to a conception of creation which exorcises some of the more unfortunate elements of Neo-platonism from the tradition. It is better if we do not speak of creation as divine self-communication, which is more appro-priately used of God's self-giving in Christ. This is because a general rather than particular divine self-communication runs the risk of an essentially Neoplatonist, emanationist, and finally pantheist absorption of the creature in the Creator. In other words, if we understand the creation rather than Christ as the locus of God's giving of himself, we are in danger of losing the essential otherness of creation from the Creator, that which it needs to have if it is truly to be itself in distinction from God.[48] The point of stressing a trinitarian way of construing the relation of Creator and creation is that it enables us to understand both the past and the continuing creative divine agency toward the world without closing the space between God and the created order. The doctrine of creation has to do, that is to say, with the establishment of the other in its own distinctive reality: not divine self-

---

[46] J. W. Trigg remarks that Origen's 'doctrine of creation out of nothing ultimately provides for an eschatology more consistent with Platonism than the new heaven and earth of the Bible'. *Origen. The Bible and Philosophy in the Third Century Church* (Atlanta: John Knox, 1983), p. 110.

[47] Basil of Caesarea, *On the Holy Spirit*, XV. 36 and 38.

[48] This point might hold also against Moltmann's tendency to conceive creation out of nothing as an act of divine kenosis or self-emptying.

communication, but divine constituting of the world to be truly other, and so itself. If that be causality, then we can continue to use the concept, but only if that carries connotations of personal, willed, intentional, consistent and loving agency.[49]

[49] I am grateful to Paul Metzger for pointing out some errors and raising some questions which have helped me to clarify some of the points made in this paper.

5. *Creatio ex Nihilo* and the Spatio-Temporal Dimensions, with special reference to Jürgen Moltmann and D. C. Williams

Alan J. Torrance

Few books in recent years have done more to initiate and inspire discussion of the doctrine of creation than Jürgen Moltmann's Gifford Lectures 1984–5.[1] Central to the argument of this book is a series of suppositions about the nature of space and time which conditions and informs his interpretation of the doctrine of 'creation out of nothing'. After considering the elements in Jürgen Moltmann's approach which encourage him to adopt these suppositions, I shall go on to offer a critique of the understanding of space and time which so shapes his approach. Finally, in the third part of this paper, I shall consider how certain central and widely held assumptions about the doctrine of *creatio ex nihilo* require substantial reconstruction – reconstruction which serves the broader theological task in a number of ways.

Moltmann opens his exposition of the doctrine with an analysis of the 'priestly' creation narratives from which he derives two fairly innocuous, although important, traditional theological affirmations, namely: (1) that there is a self-distinction on the part of God from the 'created' world and (2) that the world from which God distinguishes himself in the creative act is nonetheless desired by him – 'the world is not in itself divine; nor is it an emanation from God's eternal being'. It is, however, 'the specific outcome of his decision of will'. Consequently, since heaven and earth are the result of God's creative activity, they are 'neither divine nor demonic, neither eternal like God himself, nor meaningless and futile. They are contingent.'[2]

---

[1] These were published in 1985 under the title, *God in Creation: an Ecological Doctrine of Creation* (London: SCM Press, 1985).

[2] Moltmann, *God in Creation*, pp. 72–3.

The later emergence in Judaism of the interpretation of creation as a creation *out of nothing* rather than merely the bestowal of order on a prior state of chaos is a consistent development of this theology. It suggests that: 'Wherever and whatever God creates is without any preconditions. There is no external necessity which occasions his creativity, and no inner compulsion which could determine it. Nor is there any primordial matter whose potentiality is pre-given to his creative activity, and which would set him material limits.'[3] In sum, the doctrine of creation out of nothing emphasises that creation is unconditioned. It denotes a radically free and sovereign act on the part of God.

In affirming the doctrine, the question may emerge whether the phrase *ex nihilo* does not itself suggest some kind of conditioning ontology of nothingness. In their various discussions, both Otto Weber and Jürgen Moltmann call on the distinction between *nihil privatum* and *nihil negativum* which derives from the *Timaeus* and also the traditional Platonic distinctions between *me on* (the relative negation of being) and *ouk on* (the absolute negation of being) in order to offer a formulation of the doctrine which obviates any potential inconsistency here.[4] For our purposes, however, all that is required is that we reiterate Moltmann's comment that the phrase '*ex nihilo*' intends to say nothing more than that 'the world was created neither out of pre-existent matter, nor out of the divine Being itself'.

I   Creation out of Nothing and the Nature–Will Dilemma

The aforementioned affirmations are distilled by Moltmann into two central theses which are fundamental to his discussion but which he also perceives as generating a problematic tension. This he seeks to resolve by way of a panentheistic ontology. It is this which will be the focus of our critique. Moltmann's two central theses are as follows: first, creation was 'called into existence by the free will of God'. It is *e libertate Dei*.[5] Second, creation is not simply, however, a demonstration of boundless power; it is the communication of God's love which knows neither premises nor preconditions. It is also, therefore, *ex amore Dei*. The predicate *ex nihilo* serves to emphasise the ultimacy and unconditioned nature of the divine love.

[3] Moltmann, *God in Creation*, p. 74.
[4] Otto Weber, *Foundations of Dogmatics, Volume One,* translated by Darrell Guder (Grand Rapids: Eerdmans, 1981), p. 501.
[5] Moltmann, *God in Creation*, p. 75.

The essential thrust of his argument is to suggest, therefore, that creation is an ecstatic act of the eternal divine communion whose ultimate goal or *telos* is the communion of the Kingdom of God.[6] That a concept of communion does indeed underlie the Old Testament interpretation of creation is evidenced in the covenant conceptuality which shapes the redaction of the earlier creation narratives.[7] Consequently, just as God's covenant relationship to Israel is unilateral, unconditional and unconditioned, creation must be construed in the same terms. *Creatio ex nihilo* expresses precisely that. No theologian has emphasised the integral connection between creation and covenant more strongly than Karl Barth. Furthermore, when we consider 2 Maccabees 7.23 (which has traditionally – if, perhaps, incorrectly[8] – been considered to be the first explicit expression of creation 'out of nothing') we find further testimony to the intrinsic connection made in the Jewish tradition between the doctrine of creation and what might be described as the category of communion. The story relates to the Syrian oppression of the Jews where we find a distressed mother seeking to console her seven sons who are being tortured and killed one after the other – 'it was not I who gave you life and set you in your bodily frames. It is the Creator of the universe who moulds man at his birth and plans the origin of all things.' The suggestion is that the God who is responsible for all things, values his creation and will not ultimately allow his purposes of communion to be negated by circumstances and events foreign to these. The implication is that the oppressive activities of the Syrians will not have the final word.

If both Barth and Moltmann are eager to affirm an integral connection between the doctrine of creation out of nothing and what one might refer to as an ontology of communion, it is also at this point that their interpretations begin to diverge and to

---

[6] Moltmann, *God in Creation*, p. 81.

[7] As Bernhard Anderson argues in his introductory essay to *Creation in the Old Testament*, the first dimension of Israel's creation faith concerns the creation of a people as this is articulated in the Mosaic covenant tradition (pp. 3–7). And at the heart of the Genesis creation account, he comments, 'the narrator ... portrays the transcendence that arises from the social nature of human beings: "Ein Mensch ist kein Mensch" ("A single human being is not human at all"), as the German proverb goes. In this story ... creation is the coming to be of *adam* – human being that is made for community in which life is given in relation to God and in relation to the other, the partner' (p. 7). 'Mythopoeic and Theological Dimensions of Biblical Creation Faith', in *Creation in the Old Testament*, ed. Bernhard Anderson (London: SPCK, 1984), pp. 1–24.

[8] Cf. Gerhard May, *Creatio ex Nihilo: the Doctrine of 'Creation out of Nothing' in Early Christian Thought*, translated by A. S. Worrall (Edinburgh: T. & T. Clark, 1994), pp. 6–8.

do so quite substantially. Moltmann discerns in Barth what he describes (not only here but elsewhere) as a 'Nominalist fringe' pointing to a latent monarchianism in his doctrine of God. This is expressed in Barth's unqualified emphasis on divine freedom – the freedom of God not only to create but also to reveal himself. When Barth suggests that 'God ... could have remained satisfied with Himself and with the impassible glory and blessedness of His own inner life',[9] Moltmann believes this seriously undermines a proper theology of the love of God and God's purposes of communion with the created order.[10]

Associating Barth with the Reformed doctrine of the eternal decrees, Moltmann is determined to reject any talk of creation as a resolve of God's *will* rather than a resolve of God's *being*. Neither creation, nor, indeed, revelation may be seen as arbitrary expressions of some divine will or 'freedom of choice' the quintessence of which, he argues, is 'almighty power' or 'the absolute right of disposition over property'. Rather, creation and the history of God's dealings with the created order must be the expression and communication of a divine love that cannot do otherwise.[11]

Second, Moltmann argues, both in *God in Creation* and also in *The Trinity and the Kingdom of God*, that the notion of a divine decision of will involves 'introducing into the essential nature of God the before–after structure which belongs to every decision of this kind'.[12] This, in turn, leads us to ask about that which was 'before' in God which led to the decision, that is, about the divine nature, and whether this determined the decision or whether the decision was entirely arbitrary.[13]

[9] Moltmann, *God in Creation*, p. 82.
[10] Cf. his earlier book, The *Trinity and the Kingdom of God: The Doctrine of God*, translated by Margaret Kohl (London: SCM Press, 1981), p. 53, where he asks: 'What concept of liberty is Barth applying to God here? Is this concept of absolute freedom of choice not a threat to God's truth and goodness? Could God really be content with his "impassible glory"? Does God really not need those whom in the suffering of his love he loves unendingly?' [*Trinität und Reich Gottes: Zur Gotteslehre*, München, 1980, p. 68.]
[11] One wonders, however, what he himself means when he suggested that 'before God creates the world he determines that he will be the world's Creator' (*God in Creation*, pp. 79–80). Might this 'determination' not be regarded as a 'decision of will' or, indeed, a 'decree'?
[12] Moltmann, *God in Creation*, p. 82. Cf. *The Trinity and the Kingdom of God*, 'If the eternal origin of the creative and suffering love of God is seen as lying in God's decision of will, then time's "beforehand – afterwards" structure has to be carried into the divine eternity as well; and we have to talk about a divine nature *before* this decision and a divine nature *after* it. There would be no other way of defining the decision more closely' (pp. 53–4).
[13] See also Moltmann's critique of interpretations of creation which make exclusive recourse to the concept of the divine will in *The Trinity and the Kingdom of God*, pp. 111–14.

This, of course, amounts to a somewhat anthropomorphic projection into God of the old determinist argument utilised against libertarianism. The obvious retort, of course, is to argue that if God's 'ecstatic act of creation' is simply an outworking of some essential creativity in the divine nature then it cannot be meaningful to distinguish between the divine *hypostasis* and the divine *ekstasis*. The two collapse into each other and the very concept of creativity, not to mention *ekstasis*, dissolves. God is then reduced to an infinite process and the created order to a mere moment in the necessary operations of some absolute organism. Ironically, Moltmann's fear of projecting a 'before and after' into God (as this is assumed, he believes, by the concept of a free decision of the divine will) can lead, all too easily, to an approach which *itself* temporalises God and absolutises a temporally conceived process of creation. The result of any such move will, again, be a doctrine of the *aeternitas mundi*.

These are, of course, old debates and Moltmann is not unaware of these long-standing dilemmas. Consequently, it is to his attempt to avoid these and to find a coherent way forward that we must now turn. Moltmann is quite clear that he does not wish to identify himself with the kind of process theology deriving from Whitehead's thought – in his view, 'process theology of this kind has no doctrine of creation'. 'It is conversant', he writes, 'only with a doctrine about the preservation and ordering of the world.'[14] For similar reasons, he is also concerned to reject Gnostic or Neoplatonic doctrines of emanation where creation is conceived as simply an 'overflow of the divine nature'.[15] Such an approach he finds in Tillich where the 'divine life' and the 'divine creativity' are 'one and the same thing', where the 'divine life is essentially creative and actualises itself in inexhaustible abundance' and 'God is therefore the Creator to all eternity'.[16] On this view no adequate distinction can be produced, he argues, between 'God's creatures and God's eternal creation of himself'.[17] What, he asks, distinguishes this from 'the pantheism of *natura naturans*?'[18] But on the other hand, Moltmann also rejects, as we have already seen, the Reformed doctrine of a divine decree. Over and against these two options he determines to find a 'deeper alternative'. If the truth of the decrees is that creation is the outcome of God's decision and if the truth of the doctrine

[14] Moltmann, *God in Creation*, p. 79.
[15] Moltmann, *God in Creation*, p. 83.
[16] Moltmann, *God in Creation*, p. 83.
[17] Moltmann, *God in Creation*, p. 84.
[18] Moltmann, *God in Creation*, p. 84.

of emanation is that the divine life discloses itself, then, he suggests, 'we must say that God discloses himself in the decision he makes'.[19] His divine life flows into his resolve, and from that resolve overflows to his creatures. Through the resolve, the divine life is communicated to created beings. This involves a becoming in God that does not detract from the divine – 'through its resolve, the divine life becomes creative' and yet, he adds, 'in its creativity it is wholly and entirely itself, and is itself wholly and entirely'.[20]

It is in these terms that Moltmann seeks to escape the freedom–nature dilemma. God is entirely free when he is entirely himself. He is not entirely free, therefore, when he can do and leave undone what he likes. An all-embracing trinitarian doctrine of creation conceived in these terms will, he suggests, take us beyond these traditional dilemmas between divine freedom and divine nature, beyond the alternatives of decree and emanation, and will thereby transcend the dichotomy between 'God as absolute subject' and 'God as supreme substance'.

II Moltmann's Solution: a Panentheist, Kenotic Protology

So how precisely will an 'all-embracing trinitarian doctrine' accomplish this? For Moltmann, the answer is to be found in the Jewish, kabbalistic doctrine of God's 'self-limitation', that is of a divine *zimsum*, as expounded by Isaac Luria.[21] He appeals, in other words, to what we might term a 'kenotic protology'. The beginning of all things is an act of divine contraction. Before God issues creatively out of himself, he acts inwardly on himself in an act of self-limitation. This is essential if a God who is omnipresent is to engage in an act of creation that is 'outward'. He comments, 'Theologians have made [the] distinction between God's "inward" and his "outward" aspect so much a matter of course that no one has even asked the critical question: can the omnipotent God have an "outward" aspect at all? . . . If there were a realm outside God, God would not be omnipresent.' For Moltmann, there is, indeed, only one possible way of conceiving an *extra Deum*. 'In order to create a world "outside" himself, the infinite God must have made room beforehand for a finitude in himself.'[22]

---

[19] Moltmann, *God in Creation*, p. 85.
[20] Moltmann, *God in Creation*, p. 85.
[21] Moltmann, *God in Creation*, p. 87. His approach is anticipated in his earlier discussion of God's self-limitation and creation in *The Trinity and the Kingdom of God*, pp. 108ff.
[22] Moltmann, *God in Creation*, pp. 86–7.

Three propositions summarise different aspects of this theory:

1. 'God makes room for his creation by withdrawing his presence.'[23] It is only through 'the yielding up of the *nihil* that a *creatio ex nihilo* is conceivable at all'.[24]

2. God 'withdraws himself from himself to himself' in order to make creation possible. 'His creative activity outwards is preceded by this humble divine self-restriction.'

3. But third, 'if creation *ad extra* takes place in the space freed by God himself, then ... the reality outside God still remains *in* the God who has yielded up that "outwards" in himself'.[25]

The core of Moltmann's third way, therefore, is that *creatio ex nihilo* is an act of will outwards precisely because there has been a prior, inner, substantial change in God wherein God vacates the space in which creation is to take place. However, although this vacated space ceases to *be* God he also wishes to emphasise that it remains '*in* God'. Now whether this solves the nature–will dilemma remains unclear. Are we not entitled to suppose that this divine contraction presupposes a logically prior resolve on God's part to contract in this manner? And it is not immediately clear that the fact that he speaks of a contraction on the part of the divine substance means that such an explanation may not also be taken to presuppose some 'freedom of choice' on God's part.

This debate aside, however, there are some positive and, indeed, appealing elements to such an interpretation. Creation is portrayed in a manner that contrasts dramatically with deistically conceived notions of arbitrary, divine fabrication. The suggestion of a divine event that is not merely extrinsic to God but involves an ontological 'becoming' on the part of God radically undermines any inclination to interpret creation as related to God in arbitrary or merely 'external' ways. Second, this kind of exposition stresses the continuity between creation and the incarnation. The 'self-emptying' of God in the incarnation is not now simply to be seen as an event which

---

[23] 'What comes into being is a *nihil* ... which represents the partial negation of the divine Being, inasmuch as God is not yet Creator.' This space is, by its very nature, a 'God-forsaken space'. This he then describes as hell, absolute death, though he then qualifies this by adding 'Admittedly the *nihil* only acquires this menacing character through the self-isolation of created beings to which we give the name of sin and godlessness.' Moltmann, *God in Creation*, p. 88.

[24] Moltmann, *God in Creation*, p. 88.

[25] Moltmann, *God in Creation*, pp. 88–9.

takes place 'out of the blue'. Rather, the divine 'contraction' in love at Bethlehem and on the cross is the culmination and fulfilment of precisely that dynamic which is constitutive of the very event of creation. Christian theology in its entirety may be seen, therefore, to be an integrated articulation of a divine *becoming* on the part of God – making the doctrine of the incarnation (and, indeed, of Pentecost) no more strange or 'counter-intuitive' than that of creation. This is not to mention a further apparent virtue, namely, the inherent 'political correctness' of such an approach – Moltmann refers to the so-called 'motherly categories'[26] of withdrawing and 'letting be' and the whole theory is suggestive of creation's taking place within a divine womb. All this might seem to suggest a new and more appealing way of thinking about the creation event than traditional models have offered.

Some difficult and important questions, however, require to be addressed here. It would seem that, despite the various possible interpretations of Moltmann's word-plays, his panentheistic interpretation suggests that space is not *created* but, rather, *vacated*. Its vacation is temporally *prior*, moreover, to the creation event. There are, it would seem, two distinct events, therefore – a *vacatio ex Deo* or *vacatio a Deo* where this is not to be conceived as a creative event and *then* a *creatio in spatio*. This, however, gives rise to two obvious issues – the first relating to the nature of space and the second to the nature of time.

1. Is creation spatially located?

Moltmann seems to operate with a concept of absolute space, interpreting God's omnipresence as infinite and absolute space-occupancy. The divine omnipresence then becomes limited or conditioned in the contraction prior to creation. This is because, for Moltmann, space is *vacated* rather than *created*. What seems to inform his thinking is what T. F. Torrance has described, in a very different context, as a 'container' or 'receptacle' model of space rather than the more relational and dynamic conceptions of spatiality suggested by scientific developments since Newton.[27]

Moreover, Moltmann's concern with the 'where' of creation and his *seemingly* literal interpretation of the spatial metaphors inherent in the '*ad extra*' language, for example, appear

---

26 Moltmann, *God in Creation*, p. 88.
27 See T. F. Torrance, *Space, Time and Incarnation* (Oxford: Oxford University Press, 1969), pp. 38ff. He writes, 'Newton himself spoke of space and time as an infinite receptacle in terms of the infinity and eternity of God, for it is in God as in a container that we live and move and have our being' (p. 38).

to commit him to a panentheism that suggests not only a container model of space but a container model of God. One might add here, that his own metaphorical language usage and word-plays do not always clarify precisely how he intends us to conceive of the creation event. Might it be, for example, that the 'en' of his pan*en*theism is to be understood not literally as a spatial '*en*' but, rather, as a more generally *ontological* 'en'? If so, then his panentheism may not be as irretrievably committed to container models of space and/or God as we are implying? (This, of course, begs the question as to whether, on his argument, one can have the latter without the former.) It is far from clear, however, that we can get Moltmann off the hook by suggesting that his language here is essentially metaphorical. His argument, for example, that a spatial vacation on the part of God is necessary for the non-divine to exist due to God's omnipresence seems to suggest otherwise. If, indeed, he *is* arguing for such a literal form of pan-en-theism (and there is continual ambiguity in his discussion) one is left asking whether this really is more theologically satisfactory than a rather less complicated Christian 'the-en-panism', that is, that by the Spirit, God is freely and ecstatically present in, to and for the created order.

2. *Is creation temporally located?*

Our second area of criticism concerns the much more difficult and, indeed, much more important question as to how Moltmann conceives of the relationship between time and creation. We have suggested that he would appear to operate with a concept of absolute space. The thrust of his discussion would also seem to suggest that he operates with a concept of absolute (indeed, linear) time as well. His panentheistic exposition speaks of a history in God – a process that continues prior to creation, through creation and culminates in the Kingdom of God. His views here have led critics to comment that his theology is essentially a form of process theology. And his exposition of the doctrine of creation does indeed appear to require a pre-creation history in God. He argues, for example, that creation is founded on God's creative resolve which is 'an act of will that is directed both outwards and inwards, whereby the act that is directed inwards *objectively precedes* the divine act that is turned outwards: before God creates the world he determines that he will be the world's Creator'.[28]

Now it may again be argued that the temporal expressions he uses are being applied here metaphorically. But he cannot

---

[28] Moltmann, *God in Creation*, pp. 79–80 (my italics).

be defended so easily when he identifies *creatio ex nihilo* with *creatio originalis* and then strongly differentiates between *creatio originalis* and *creatio continua* – where 'continuous creation' denotes God's sustaining and preserving activity through time, as this projects toward the *creatio nova*.

He writes, 'We might say that [at] every moment the Creator reiterates his primal Yes, and repeats both his creative and his ordering activity. God does not create anything new but creates unremittingly what he once created by sustaining and preserving it.'[29] Such distinctions may only be made, however, on the supposition that creation takes place in and through (during) time. That this is indeed his view is evident when he goes on to say:

> Theological tradition has laid a one-sided stress on the preservation of the world: *conservatio mundi*. In the new theologies of evolution and process, a one-sided stress is laid on the world's development. But if we discover the *creatio continua* between the *creatio originalis* and the *nova creatio*, we shall perceive the unremitting creative activity of God as an activity that both preserves *and* innovates.

The concern here is that, in common with much of the tradition, Moltmann identifies *creatio ex nihilo* with a temporally original creation of an initial state of affairs and set of conditions – an event which follows earlier events in God. And this temporally original creative active act is then followed by (and to be distinguished from) the further time-bound process of God's continuous, creative preservation, moment by moment, of what was created at the beginning of time.

Despite the fact that this kind of picture may seem to fit with the everyday supposition of absolute, linear time, it is of some theological importance to ask if this is consistent with an appropriate description of *creatio ex nihilo* – or whether, indeed, it does not lead to a somewhat mythological conception of God where God and humanity participate in some absolute, common, temporal process. The entire conceptuality suggests, and would appear to derive from, fallacious adherence to what the Harvard philosopher D. C. Williams and the Australian philosopher J. J. C. Smart, among others, refer to as the 'myth of passage'. The 'myth of passage' denotes the assumption that either we move through time or that time itself moves – that

---

[29] And further, he writes, a 'detailed doctrine of the *creatio continua* must see God's historical activity under [two] aspects: the preservation of the world he has created, and the preparation of its completion and perfecting. The historical activity of God stands between initial creation and the new creation.' Moltmann, *God in Creation*, p. 209.

there is some absolute passage of time from past to future or some absolute passage of the experiencing subject through time. The theological counterpart of this is the view that there is an absolute and overarching temporal process with recourse to which we may interpret the history of God and his dealings with humanity. Unless we operate with such a model, the distinction between *creatio ex nihilo* and *creatio continua* becomes meaningless and the concept of a temporally original creation and the identification of this with *creatio ex nihilo* seriously confused.

III   D. C. Williams' Critique of the Myth of Passage[30]

In everyday life we tend to assume that time passes and that we move through time. We say that 'time flows or flies or marches, that hours pass by and years roll on'. Integral to this way of thinking is the supposition that 'reality' denotes exclusively 'that which inhabits the present'. We assume what Williams describes as a 'surge of presentness' which is interpreted to be nothing less than the very 'boon of existence itself'. Time is assumed to denote a unique and essential movement from past to future and 'reality' refers exclusively to that which is 'present'. This leads us to think of time as reifying 'minute by minute a limbo of unthings'.[31] And simultaneously, it condemns that which is fleetingly now, and thus real, to a limbo of past unreality, the very instant that what is now present has become past. The domain of the real, therefore, denotes exclusively all that is present and which, therefore, is continually moving forward into the future. This model leads us to assume that there was once an original event of creation out of nothing but that we now have another kind of divine activity which is the continuing preservation and sustaining of things in the reality of the ever-moving present.

Over against this whole conceptuality or ontology, Williams established that the assumption that time flows or moves, or that we (together with all other existents) move through time in some sense, is simply confused. The supposition that the very essence of reality is bound up with some kind of temporal movement

---

[30] The following discussion is based on D. C. Williams' profoundly important article, 'The Myth of Passage', *The Journal of Philosophy*, Volume XLVIII, No. 15, July 19, 1951, pp. 457–72. Despite the remarkable impact which this article has had on the philosophy of time, theologians have failed to take any account of Williams' arguments.

[31] 'The Myth of Passage', p. 462. I might add that Williams sees a difference of emphasis between the Augustinian account and the contemporary focus – he comments that Augustine 'pictures the present as passing into the past, where the modern pictures the present as invading the future' (ibid).

whereby future events which are unreal (because they are in the future) become real and then instantaneously pass into history, thereby ceasing to be real, is demonstrably false.

Williams' basic argument is quite simple. If time flows past us or if we move through time, then we are obliged to postulate a hypertime with respect to which this motion or movement takes place.[32] This is because motion is always motion with respect to time – motion or passage are themselves temporal concepts. If time itself moves it must move with recourse to some higher level of time. J. J. C. Smart expresses it in this way, 'If motion in space is feet per second, at what speed is the flow of time? Seconds per what? Moreover, if passage is of the essence of time, it is presumably the essence of hypertime, too, which would lead us to postulate a hyper-hypertime and so on *ad infinitum*.'[33] In other words, there is no meaningful respect in which time moves or flows or that we, or any other identities for that matter, advance through time. To attempt to do this is to double one's world by assuming different levels of temporality. And this immediately commits one to an infinitely regressive process of explanation.

A much more adequate way to think about time, Williams argues, is to conceive of it in terms of a world 'manifold of occurrences' (p. 470). This suggests that, instead of our thinking of the identities of things in three-dimensional terms as 'moving' through time, we conceive of the identities of things within a four-dimensional spatio-temporal framework. In terms of this 'theory of the manifold', all that is is conceived *not* as having some kind of three-dimensional (or indeed, spiritual) reality which moves through time but rather as four-dimensionally extended realities which require to be described in four-dimensional terms.[34] To be real is to be a spatio-temporally extended reality with a four-dimensional identity. And four-dimensional identities are denoted by means of cross-spatial and cross-temporal co-ordinates. The identity of Alan Torrance, therefore, would be plotted four-dimensionally com-

[32] Here I am utilising J. J. C. Smart's tight summary of Williams' argument in his article on 'Time' in Paul Edwards, *Encyclopaedia of Philosophy*, vol. 8 (London: Collier-Macmillan, 1967), p. 126.
[33] Smart, 'Time', p. 126.
[34] Williams writes: 'I believe that the universe consists, without residue, of the spread of events in space–time, and that if we thus accept realistically the four-dimensional fabric of juxtaposed actualities we can dispense with all those dim non-factual categories which have so bedevilled our race: the potential, the subsistential, and the influential, the noumenal, the numinous, and the non-natural. But I am arguing here, not that there is nothing outside the natural world of events, but that the theory of the manifold is anyhow literally true and adequate to that world' (p. 458).

bining spatio-temporal co-ordinates which include both those of his birth as well as those of his death – despite the fact that, at the time of writing this paper, this has not yet occurred![35] In sum, it is false to think that we move through time. We are simply temporally extended beings with thoughts and feelings all of which occupy different spatio-temporal places.

All this challenges us to distinguish between the harmless metaphors of everyday experience (or existential phenomenology), on the one hand, and theological, metaphysical or ontological description which make claims about the nature of reality, the nature of creation and, indeed, the being of God in the event of creation, on the other. In other words, we must refuse to move from the plethora of expressions which appear to denote temporal passage to a theological, metaphysical or ontological endorsement of some absolute temporal passage.

The essential point here is made by Williams as follows:

> Nothing can 'move' in time alone any more than in space alone, and time itself cannot 'move' any more than space itself. 'Does this road go anywhere?' asks the city tourist. 'No, it stays right along here,' replies the countryman. Time 'flows' only in the sense in which a line flows or a landscape 'recedes into the west'. That is, it is an ordered extension. And each of us proceeds through time only as a fence proceeds across a farm: that is, parts of our being, and the fence's, occupy successive instants and points, respectively. There is passage, but it is nothing extra. It is the mere happening of things, their strung-along-ness in the manifold.[36]

As soon as we try to add to the theory of the four-dimensional manifold the 'extra' idea of temporal passage we immediately double our world, he argues, by re-introducing terms like 'moving' and 'becoming' in a sense which both requires and forbids coherent interpretation.[37] There are a number of reasons which help to explain why we are so easily misled here. Space restricts us to mentioning two.

1. Non-parallelism between spatial and temporal reality

The first factor is the apparent non-parallelism between spatial and temporal reality which leads us to think that there cannot be temporal extension in the way that there is spatial

---

[35] To conceive of a person literally as some kind of non-temporal ego whose reality belongs exclusively to the 'now', i.e. to some infinitely non-extended present moment, and who is being helplessly swept along through time to her annihilation is essentially confused – despite the fact that due to our strung-out-ness in time we find we cannot help but think in this way.

[36] Williams, 'The Myth of Passage', p. 463.

[37] Williams, 'The Myth of Passage', p. 463.

THE DOCTRINE OF CREATION

extension. Reality, it is assumed, is constituted of spatially
extended things in a non-extended, moving 'now'.

St. Augustine gave much consideration to what he perceived
to be the non-parallelisms between spatial and temporal
extension. Firstly, he was puzzled by the fact that, whereas we
can compare two different spatial lengths with the same ruler,
we cannot measure time in the same way. We cannot, that is,
measure two different processes at different times with the
same temporal movement of my watch. It takes two different
movements of my watch hand and at every point of observation
and comparison part of the process which one is measuring
has passed away. One can never, therefore, have all of both
temporal extensions before you at once, as one can when
comparing different spatial extensions.[38] A related puzzle
regarding temporal extension emerges, for Augustine, in the
attempt to make sense of speaking of a 'long' period of time
and, therefore, any period of time at all. In Book XI of his
Confessions, Chapter 15, he argues that 'the present has no
extension whatever'. The argument is that if it is extended at
all then it can be divided into the part that is future and the
part that is past. Clearly, this leads to the view that past
identities do not exist to the extent that they are 'no longer'
and future identities similarly do not exist to the extent that
they are 'not yet'. This, in turn, leads to the assumption that
the totality of existence is to be identified with occupancy of an
infinitely non-extended, indivisible 'now'.

Such puzzles serve, apparently, to add support to the view
that temporality is to be conceived in terms of the continual
movement of an infinitely non-extended 'now' – extension being
assumed to typify spatial reality in radical contradistinction to
the temporal. A moment's thought, however, is sufficient to
make clear that there is no more an infinitely non-extended
'now' in time than there is an infinitely non-extended 'here' in
space.[39]

2. The Indo-European system of tenses

A second source of confusion in our thinking about reality and
hence about creation is that our forms of thought tend to be

---

[38] Cf. J. J. C. Smart's discussion of this in his article 'Time', in Paul Edwards,
Encyclopaedia of Philosophy, vol. 8 (London: Collier-Macmillan, 1967), p.
126, from which I have drawn in this summary.

[39] As Ludwig Wittgenstein suggests in *The Blue Book*, the problem here is, at
least in part, one of grammar. The conflict between two different usages of
the word 'measure' when used of time and space leads one to ask, with
Augustine, 'What is time?' which is essentially the wrong question. Cf.
*The Blue and Brown Books: Preliminary Studies for the 'Philosophical
Investigations'* (Oxford: Blackwell, 1958), p. 26.

linked too closely to the Indo-European tense system of verbs which locks reference to the reality of things into a system of tenses. Consequently, in order to assert the reality of something we are obliged to use words which are temporally indexical or reflexive in expression. To affirm the existence of an identity involves utilising the present tense of the verb 'to exist'. This has the effect of 'locking' the totality of all that possesses reality into the reference of the indexical 'now'. This, in turn, leads us to think that for something to be 'real' it must occupy some supposed 'space of time' between the past and the future – further confirming the tendency to attach exclusive reality to the present, to the immediate. This way of thinking makes it seem counter-intuitive to suggest that realities which extend into the future are the objects of *creatio ex nihilo*. This further inclines us to locate *creatio ex nihilo* at the beginning of history due to the resulting tendency to interpret present events synchronously, or synchronistically, in the light of their relations to the past. Given that we assume that there was a time when the whole expanse of time was 'in the future', 'not yet' and therefore absolutely unreal or non-existent, we are led to project *creatio ex nihilo* backwards in time such that it concerns temporally original events and initial conditions and is reserved exclusively for them. The consequence of this way of thinking about 'reality' is that it seems natural (indeed, necessary) for us to identify *creatio ex nihilo* with *creatio originalis* – thereby *locating creation itself within time*!

Clearly, this confusion would be considerably less likely to arise if we operated, as we ought, with two forms of the verb 'to be'. The first would function in a non-temporally-indexical manner resembling the use of the existential quantifier (affirming the existence of identities whose time occupancy is not necessarily simultaneous with the affirming or performing of the proposition). The second form would utilise tense and thereby operate indexically to refer to events in such a way that specific reference was made to the temporally located perspective of the person making the utterance.

'There *will be* a train strike next week!' would more properly be 'There *is* (first form of the verb 'to be') a train strike which is temporally located the week after this statement is (second form of the verb 'to be') being made!' A still more 'objective', non-indexical form would affirm the reality of the train strike and provide its spatio-temporal location simply by utilising a series of space-time co-ordinates which made no appeal to the location of the affirmation of the existential statement itself.

The purpose of this argumentation is to suggest that it is theologically misleading and ontologically distortive to identify

creatio ex nihilo with *creatio originalis* (and thereby to distinguish it from *creatio continua*) or to interpret creation as
either located in time or extended in time. To suggest that it is
ushers into theology a series of further errors which distort
other doctrines.

If we are to understand the relation of the Creator to the
created order in an integrated and integrative manner it is
imperative that God not be thought of as creating objects in
space or spatial objects in time. Rather, we are required to
think in terms of God's creating the totality of spatio-temporal
identities together with their interconnective matrices from
absolutely nothing. If we do not approach creation in this
manner then we find ourselves attaching spatial or temporal
conditions to *creatio ex nihilo*, as Jürgen Moltmann can now be
seen to have done.

An appropriately conceived doctrine of *creatio ex nihilo*
will advocate neither a doctrine of spatial vacation which
absolutises space nor any approach which suggests an overarching, absolute temporal process. It should, moreover, be
clear that it is as inappropriate to distinguish *creatio ex nihilo*
from *creatio continua* as it is to think in terms of an absolute,
linear, temporal process which extends beyond the created
order into the divine. Indeed, it is as confused to suggest that
God's creative activity is temporally extended in this way as it
is to suggest that it is spatially extended. To distinguish *creatio
continua* from *creatio ex nihilo* or to identify *creatio ex nihilo*
with *creatio originalis* is technically as absurd as it is to plot
God's creative activity spatially. That is, it is no less absurd
than if I were to argue that God started creating right in the
middle (as he had to) and is in the process of working outwards
since *creatio ex nihilo* must necessarily denote the absolute
middle of space! There is no more a *creatio originalis*, conceived
in these terms, than there is a *creatio in medio* and there is no
more a *creatio continua* than there is a *creatio extensa*.[40]

Unfortunately, all these confusions come to expression in
Jürgen Moltmann's panentheistic account of creation – that
is, his supposedly 'trinitarian' solution to the will–nature
dilemma. By contrast, a theological doctrine of *creatio ex nihilo*
should, as we have suggested, interpret God as creating space–
time *per se*, the entire spatio-temporal nexus, the totality of all

[40] Professor Christoph Schwöbel (in his contribution to this volume) uses the
expression 'continued creation' instead of 'continuous creation' – a *creatio
continuata* in place of *creatio continua*. However, 'continued creation' is no
less guilty of suggesting that creation is extended in time than 'continuous
creation'. Creation is simply not an infra-temporal event and nothing is to be
served by conceiving of it as such.

that is, together with the ordering and inter-relating matrices constitutive of the totality of created identities. In other words, God creates the space-time manifold *ex nihilo*.

V Conclusion

Where does all this lead? How important is this kind of ontological accuracy of description (if that is what it is) when we are seeking to describe the mystery of creation?

There are a number of central theological issues for which the removal of confusion here is profoundly significant.

First, a dimensional view of time of the kind advocated by Williams undermines the latent deism which derives all too easily from a confused temporal locating of the creation event at t^1 on some supposed time line. Any such temporal circumscribing of the event of creation leads to an interpretation of future events as mediated by hosts of derivative events of various kinds. The effect of this is to distance the event of creation from realities further down the 'time line' which are then perceived as created only in a general and, indeed, remote sense. Consequently, the specific divine intentionality in creation fails to be related directly to particular existents. The implication of our critique, however, is that any such deistic distancing of the event of creation from our own created reality on temporal grounds is simply confused. When we cease to interpret the doctrine of *creatio ex nihilo* in temporally bound ways and as governed by assumptions of absolute passage then it becomes clear that the doctrine has no greater or more immediate bearing on co-ordinate t^1 (the earliest moment in time) than on co-ordinate t^{1994}. This is simply because there is absolutely no sense in which September 1994 is further removed from the event of the creation of the spatio-temporal order than t^1. Why? Because the event of creation *is not* spatio-temporally located! (One might add here that the widely held view that the Big Bang possesses special bearing on the question of the nature or character of *creatio ex nihilo* because it is a temporally original event is demonstrably confused for precisely the same reason!) In other words, a non-temporalised interpretation of *creatio ex nihilo* opens the door for a more adequate perception of the immediacy (used in its literal, non-temporal sense!) of the totality of the created order's contingency upon God's creativity and the concrete specificity of the divine intentionality *vis-à-vis* existents.

Second, a dimensional view of time should encourage us to approach the vitally important question of a hermeneutics of creation in a more coherent way than has traditionally been done. The identification of creation with a temporally original event has had the effect, particularly in the Western tradition, of supporting the nature–grace model. This it has done by suggesting that a theology of creation is 'original' (and there-fore 'foundational') in a way that christology is not. 'Nature' is thereby given priority over and against the grace of God in Christ. The effect of this has been to seek to accommodate christology within a more foundational soteriological agenda and soteriology within a hamartological perspective traced to a protological (and thus natural theological) agenda. The revision of traditional approaches to the 'location' of creation (and hence to the location of the doctrine of creation within systematic theology) demanded by a more coherent model of temporality should thus encourage careful reconsideration of the principle *gratia naturam perficit* to the extent that this has been utilised to endorse a pre-christological hermeneutic of nature under the auspices of so-called 'fundamental theology'. 'Fundamental theology' has traditionally side-lined christology, assuming that it belongs to a derivative and secondary theological domain, namely, soteriology, which is assumed to be quite distinct from, and materially irrelevant to, *so-called* 'protology'. The consequence of this Western theological architectonic is that a very different kind of primordiality is attached to Christ (that is if in this approach any is attached at all) than to the doctrine of the Creator. It is not least for these reasons that 'ktisiology' may be seen to be a more useful and less ambiguous term than 'protology', which also serves to further a second, and equally in-appropriate, traditional dichotomisation between protology and eschatology.

This is not to argue that such polarisations are justified even given the view of time which I am rejecting. They are not! What is being suggested, however, is that misconceptions of the nature of temporality and the consequent interpretation of the protological as primordial or fundamental has had the effect of relativising christology and pneumatology. This has ramifications across the whole spectrum of Christian doctrine. One consequence, for example, is that approaches to natural law and ethics have tended to operate with a less than adequately trinitarian concept of creation. This has led, in turn, to further disjunction and fragmentation not least in soteriology and anthropology. Another contemporary conse-quence has concerned the doctrine of God, where there has been an inclination in certain circles to replace the trinitarian formula with that of Creator, Redeemer and Sustainer of Life and where the persons of the Trinity are, thereby, reduced to different divine operations or functions each of which is bound to different periods of time – the term 'Father' denoting a temporally original event and 'the Holy Spirit' a continuing activity!

If *creatio ex nihilo* interprets the Triune Communion of God as 'simultaneously' and omnipresently related to the totality of spatio-temporal reality as its ground, then the search for a divinely endorsed hermeneutical key is less likely to be directed away from the person of the Logos and the Logos is more likely to be seen as proffering access to the 'fundamental' and primordial *telos* of the created order whatever the particular spatio-temporal co-ordinates of the incarnation happen to be. 'Fundamental theology' would be less likely, therefore, to be misled into side-stepping the 'information density'[41] or hermeneutical concentration that is the Logos and beside whom there is no other 'foundation'.

Third, the effect of this should be to give the theology of creation a more *central* role in theology. There are two reasons for this: first, because it undermines the kind of soteriologically oriented or christomonist theology that would interpret the events of Christ and the cross as standing between us and the creation event. It challenges the kind of *heilsgeschichtliche Theologie* which fails to see in the New Creation the focus, the fullness and the culmination of the *creation* and not a secondary, circumscribable domain of limited compass – thereby failing to grasp the irreducible integratedness of christology and a theology of creation. Second, the theology of creation comes to the fore, on this view, because we are now obliged to interpret every aspect of spatio-temporal existence and every kind of particular existent, be it an object, or a process, or a law, or any form of connectedness between events, in all their spatio-temporal particularity, as requiring to be understood as created *ex nihilo*. Every particular person in the vast complexity of the created order requires, therefore, to be interpreted in their particularity not as some eventual and infinitely mediated product of initial creative conditions but as freely, specifically and particularly created *ex nihilo* and demanding, therefore, to be interpreted and to be understood in the person of the Logos who locates himself in the midst of the spatio-temporal continuum as the one through whom and for whom all things were created.

[41] This is the expression which Dan Hardy uses in his essay 'Christ and Creation' in *The Incarnation: Ecumenical Studies in the Nicene-Constantinopolitan Creed*, edited by T. F. Torrance (Edinburgh: Handsel Press, 1981), pp. 88–110.

When Athanasius significantly describes Christ as the *topos*, the 'place' of God's engagement with creation, he was re-iterating the affirmation at the very heart of the Christian faith, that in Him we have nothing less than the *eph'hapax*, once-and-for-all, spatio-temporal location of God's concrete engagement with the totality of the spatio-temporal order. In the Johannine account, we find Jesus making the statement, 'Before Abraham was, I am' (John 8.58). This is a non-temporally-indexed, reflexive, existential statement determining who it is that is to be regarded as the hermeneutical reference point *vis-à-vis* the meaning of all created, human existence. To affirm the doctrine of *creatio ex nihilo* is thus to affirm that every facet of creation and every aspect of existence require ultimately to be interpreted in relation to God and therefore in terms of its specific concrete relations to the divine Triunity.

This may lead one to ask whether it still makes sense to speak of a New Creation (*creatio nova*). Strictly speaking, creation may not literally be described as 'old' in any temporal sense. The metaphor 'new' suggests that the Christ event and, indeed, the Body of Christ are not to be seen as organic develop-ments of some immanent process – the product of prior initial conditions. Rather, the 'new creation' is *creation* in truth, that is, creation whereby, in completion of his eternal creative purpose, God penetrates into the inner structures of creaturely existence and, in and through his creative presence, transforms the connective matrices of the human order from the inside, to the extent that they have become dysfunctional and thus distortive of the full realisation of God's creative intentions. And the metaphor of the New Humanity confirms that the New Creation is specifically creation in the Second Adam and, as such, fulfils and completes God's creative purposes for com-munion. The language of recapitulation is clearly profoundly appropriate here.

Finally, the collective effect of all the above should be to affirm, in the most radical way, that the Christian faith knows no doctrine of creation that is not a doctrine of *creatio ex nihilo* and that this doctrine demands to be articulated and inter-preted in irreducibly trinitarian ways – what Moltmann intended but, ultimately, failed to do. That is, it speaks not of some cosmological process but of the dynamic presence of the divine communion within the created order. God's presence is a free and ecstatic presence in, for and with the created order and God's purpose in this (discerned by the Spirit in and through the incarnate Son) is to bring to perfection the created order in its entirety within his own life. In this way, cosmology demands ecclesiological interpretation since at the very heart of this dynamic is found the communion of the Body of Christ – the Body of the One who alone is the Priest of the new humanity and the Priest of creation.

6. Creation and Eschatology

Daniel W. Hardy

I Introduction

To address creation without considering eschatology risks serious distortion to both topics, and restricts the scope of fundamental theological discussion at a time when it badly needs to be opened up. But the need should not be stated so negatively: we have reached the stage when the two must be taken together. Why? As we shall see, the two are intrinsically interconnected. And treating them together therefore brings into sharper focus the vast questions with which they deal.

Of course, considering them in their relation does not suggest that we will fully fathom them or their relation, now or ever; but it does establish the 'frame' in which our knowledge – and our ignorance – occur. We ourselves are situated within the field which they comprise: we have neither the overview which would provide us with a full perspective nor the fullness of information by which to say all that needs to be said about them. Here, I shall be limited to an attempt to sketch some ways in which they may best be explored.

What I propose to do is to explore ways in which to think about creation and eschatology together, and in doing so to examine the important interconnections between the two topics – those which show the intrinsic relation which they bear to each other and to God. They are deeply implicated in each other and within God's activity. But they are also different: they should not be merged or conflated, for that would lead eventually to a denial of the otherness of the two from each other and from God which conflicts with God's purpose for them.

In some respects, the exploration of creation and eschatology together resembles the attempt to understand space and time together, but it differs in that it adds substantive content – the nature of the configuration of the world and what occurs there in its trajectory to its outcome. So far as God's action is concerned, the issue, like that of space–time, forms one of the most fundamental 'refractions' through which theology needs to pass at any particular era in history in its endeavour to reconstitute itself in relation to current understanding. It is demonstrable that the topic, as one which sets out the field in which 'natural' events and God's actions occur, permeates traditional conceptions of the world, God and God's action. And the question of how far such earlier conceptions are to be sustained as normative for the present day requires not simply – or even primarily – that they be tested by reference to present understandings of space–time but that they be refracted through current conceptions of creation–eschatology and reconstituted therefrom.[1]

It would be fair to say that the topic of the relation between creation and eschatology goes unexamined in most academic inquiry today. That is not to say that the connection between creation and eschatology is denied. It functions, however, more as an undeveloped intuition, a bare grasping of the reason which Coleridge called the 'organ of the super-sensuous', through which the understanding is to be ordered.

> It is curious to mark how certainly – I may say instinctively
> – the reason has always pointed out to men the ultimate end
> of the various sciences, and how immediately afterwards
> they have set to work to realize that end.[2]

How the understanding of creation and eschatology is to be ordered – beyond the bare intuition that they are related – is what will concern us here.

II The Issue in Current Discussion

Theology today does not bristle with confidence over the task of exploring this unexamined interconnection of creation and eschatology; and they are ripe for reconsideration. As different aspects of a single dynamic, their full significance is more likely to be seen together than separately. And their content is also best seen when they are interrelated. It is these issues, their mutual significance and formation, which we will have to explore.

It should be obvious that the significance of each is strongly related to that of the other, but somewhat asymmetrically. This is seen in the modern history of the issues: for the most part, at least among theologians, the consideration of

---

[1] See D. W. Hardy, 'The Logic of Interdisciplinary Studies and the Coherence of Theology', Director's Report, Annual Report 1995, Center of Theological Inquiry, Princeton, N.J.

[2] S. T. Coleridge, *Table Talk*, edited by Carl Woodring (Princeton: Princeton University Press, 1990), vol. 1, p. 269. In this view, Coleridge follows a long tradition in English thought which finds a correlation between what was taken to be the seat of human being and divine reason.

creation has declined in modern times until recently, and eschatology more so; and now there is better prospect of recovery from this decline for creation than for eschatology. (The same has been true for the sciences, where there has been perennial concern for creation, but very little for eschatology.) And this asymmetrical decline and recovery is in no small part due to the conceptualities allowed in each. The onset of modern science – employing intensive methods more appropriate for uncovering special features of creation than contributing to broader issues – has frightened theologians into associating creation and eschatology too specifically with what is special to Christian faith, its 'inner core' as it were, particularly the new covenant in Jesus Christ. While there have been interesting reconstructions of creation and eschatology within this perspective, without effective dialogical correlation with nature (as understood by the sciences) and the general history of the world and the human race, the method remains a narrow one.[3] In general, however, theologians have severely restricted their access to creation, and therefore to eschatology.

We shall need to try to break through these difficulties. Along the way, we will employ very varied modes of access to the subjects – nature (where we must take the sciences seriously), history (where we must consider the nature of covenants very carefully), and relationship with God (where we must consider the dynamics of worship) – and some vigorous mental stretching!

III   What is Creation About?

First of all, what is 'creation' about? Within the single term creation, two notions jostle each other. And in each of them there is some ambiguity.

On the one hand, creation may refer to the universe and that which begins and sustains it. Even here, there is a difference of approach. The universe may mean the totality of the universe – in its total existence in space and time – of which the visible universe is just a tiny fraction. What we can see from the earth is 'relatively insignificant in comparison to the part which lies in our future'.[4] Or the universe can mean the

---

[3] The issue here is very serious: a 'monological' account of creation and eschatology, in which they are seen only from within the tradition of Christian faith, is inadequate without relating them dialogically to forms of understanding which arise without specific reference to the tradition.

[4] Frank Tipler, *The Physics of Immortality* (New York: Doubleday, 1994), p. x.

visible universe, that part which can be seen from earth, or
known from its traces in the present composition of the planet
and in each one of us. That is necessarily limited by what we
can see – a sphere about 20 billion light-years across – and by
what we can find of the forces which structure the universe,
macroscopically and microscopically.

Depending upon the particular concerns and disciplines
through which they are approached, one can focus on the
patterns or structure of the world, those of its space–time and
its organisation, the plant and animal world, and those of
humanity and human beings. In times past, these were seen in
mutual correlation, as integrally related through the notion of
creation; now, however, the most that is attempted is a
unification of theories which is said to be capable of describing
the universe in which we live, but only at a very fundamental
level.[5]

The visible universe is focused rather differently when we
seek these patterns as the field of relevant preconditions for
life, those characteristics of the physical universe which allow
the emergence of humankind,[6] or cultural ones which structure
the life of a people – much as mythic accounts of creation did
for early peoples. A feature common to these is that they
provide an integrated account conducive to better understanding of the physical and biological conditions of human life
and better guidance to human well-being.

On the other hand, the delineation of the conditions of the
world can be taken as more than descriptive in value. Together
or separately, they are frequently taken also as normative,
as designating states or processes which are constraints
shaping or determining existence, its structure and dynamic.
As such, they are manifestations of authorial (authoritative)
normativity which governs the world and human life. Hence, it
may be claimed, the ontology of the universe, the world and
human life shows a purposiveness in and beyond them. The
fact that there is something rather than nothing, or this state
of affairs rather than that, shows an intentionality embedded
in them.

Here again there is a difference of approach. Some, of a
naturalistic bent, seek only for universal states or processes,
what is ultimately the case with the universe, and often from a

[5] This is one major goal of modern cosmology in its search for the laws
governing the universe in its earliest moments.
[6] A close examination of these has led to the so-called 'anthropic principle' by
which it is claimed that the universe is of such a kind as to produce human
life. See J. D. Barrow and F. J. Tipler, *The Anthropic Cosmological Principle*
(Oxford: Clarendon Presss, 1986).

very narrow perspective – on the supposition that these are
the only norms for the universe. Things are as they are, and it
is sufficient – they say – to explain their order.[7] But others find
states or processes within the universe – its stability, motion
and direction – which are normative in some other way than
naturalistically. And these they consider to mediate a
constitutive authority, which needs attention in its own terms.[8]

Hence, summarising the two major options, 'creation' can
refer to any factors taken as important to the determinative
shape and purpose of the universe (total or visible), the world
and human beings, or to their mediation of an ultimate
constitutive state or agency in or beyond them.

In some modern discussion, creation is not so much a matter
of straightforward inquiry into a field (however extensive) and
its constitutive reality, as one of indirect concern. It is seen as
an issue co-present with others as their context or preconditions. Examples abound. The concern of ecology to sustain
the proper balance of nature implies context and preconditions:
what are the relations – whether static or dynamic – by which
life in the world is rendered possible?[9] In phenomenological
and theological accounts of humanity, creation is often treated
mainly, if not exclusively, as the precondition of freedom and
redemption. In theology, if one is concerned directly with such
primal features of life as freedom or salvation, creation is found
to be co-present with them as the configuration of life in the
world which makes freedom possible or which provides the
circumstances within which redemption can occur. That is how
Karl Barth, for example, can refer to creation as the 'external
basis of the covenant'.[10] We can also see the argument
presented elsewhere in this book by Robert Jenson in this
way: if theology is primarily concerned with the Trinitarian
God as purposive, creation is the condition for the realisation
of the purposes of this God, and receives its reality from the
realisation of these purposes. Beginning from widely differing
points, such examples show a common strategy – indirect
inquiry into creation, which limits consideration of creation to
those aspects which can be seen through some other primary
concern.

---

[7] The possibility of such a project, at least outside the realm of the physical
sciences, is now vigorously disputed by 'post-modernists'.
[8] 'The God most Christians have had is a God who is believed to exercise
world governance on the political model of the rule of a monarch over a
realm.' Peter C. Hodgson, *God in History* (Nashville: Abingdon Press, 1989),
p. 11.
[9] Cf. Barrow and Tipler, *The Anthropic Cosmological Principle*.
[10] Karl Barth, *Church Dogmatics* 3/1 (Edinburgh: T. & T. Clark, 1958).

IV   What is Eschatology About?

Now secondly, what is eschatology about? It is widely understood to be the study of the last things, referring to the Greek
term for 'last things' (*eschata*). In that sense, the term is
understood at two levels, cosmic and personal, the end of the
cosmos (invisible or visible), and the end of the person, what to
expect at the end (in the case of human beings death, judgement, heaven and hell), and how God provides for these
eventualities. In basic aspects, therefore, eschatology is similar
to creation, the discipline(s) concerned with the features of
existence, since it attempts to delineate the structure or order
of the end, such post-existence as there may be and the
normative authority by which these are constituted as what
they will be.

Is such a topic, however broadly considered, capable of
straightforward inquiry? It is at least notionally possible to
consider eschatology as the outcome of the preconditions for
the universe, the world and humanity – separately or as
combined in their nature and ongoing history. Understood in
that way, eschatology is the outcome of the existence, structure
and dynamic of the universe and world as anticipated in their
nature and history. As such, only in some respects is it
within the scope of the sciences. On the one hand, scientific
investigation has discovered the laws that govern matter in all
normal situations, but still not those which govern matter
under extreme conditions; and even those will not affect the
future evolution of the universe. And the well-defined laws
which scientists believe normally govern the universe allow
prediction of the future in principle, but, since 'a tiny change in
the initial situation can lead to change in the subsequent
behaviour that rapidly grows large . . . in practice, one can
predict accurately only a fairly short time in the future'.[11]

Unless one supposes that the discovery of the laws which
normally govern the universe, or of the unpredictability of
change, is regarded as a sufficient explanation, questions
remain. Just as the conditions of creation raise the question of
why they are as they are (something rather than nothing, this
rather than that), so the outcome of these conditions – in
dynamic combination – raises the question of what makes this
outcome what it will be. This is the question of what or who
makes the final state of the world what it will be – the question
of the constitutive agency of the end, whether nature, man or
God. Of course, we do not have messengers (if we except the

---

[11] Stephen Hawking, *Black Holes and Baby Universes* (New York: Bantam
Books, 1993), pp. 143, 154f.

resurrected Jesus) which have arrived from 'the end' (or post-existence) to tell us what is the case. But our understanding of the conditions of existence may at least, and is usually taken to, give us a format for conceiving what may or may not happen. That is a matter to which we shall need to devote more attention presently.

In earlier times, when the study of the world was more closely linked to its moral texture, and before the study of history alerted people so much to its complexities and con-tingencies, it was not only the physical conditions of the world and its life upon which the understanding of creation and eschatology might be built. Fundamental moral patterns were seen as present and continuing, and these too suggested the fundamental shape of the conditions of the world and the outcome in *eschata*. The characteristics of apocalyptic accounts in the Bible are not as fanciful as it is now popular to suppose: they identify the moral issues taken into account throughout history and in the final times, and show how they will be resolved.

But such views, whether those associated with scientific understanding or those having to do with moral patterns, have largely been displaced in theology. In eschatology as in creation, theologians have leaned heavily instead on indirect inquiry. Like creation, eschatology can be taken as an issue co-present with most others as the horizon in which their ultimate outcome is specified. In that sense, it is seen as indirectly present in the very characteristics of life in the world, and in the very living of life: in life, we are in death.[12] As we saw, one way of understanding creation is as an issue co-present with most others, in which their preconditions are specified. Eschatology, understood in the same way, is co-present in the present configuration of the universe, the world or humanity in two ways, as reference to the future and as an 'inner moment' of human self-understanding. Hence, eschatology is the final outcome anticipated in their coming to be as they are, in their creation, that study in which their 'post-conditions' – their final outcome – are specified. And these are also indirectly present – co-present – at any point of their existence. Following a pattern of thinking typical of phenomenological thinking, Karl Rahner speaks of it:

> Anamnesis and prognosis are among the necessary existen-tials of man . . . If the presentness of man's being includes reference to the future, then the future, while remaining truly future, is not simply spoken of in advance. It is an inner

[12] Cf. Deuteronomy 30.15 and 30.19.

moment of man and of his actual being as it is present to
him now. And so knowledge of the future, just in so far as it
is still to come, is an inner moment of the self-understanding
of man in his present hour of existence – and indeed grows
out of it.[13]

If we are not careful, however, such views make eschatology
adjectival to the self-understanding of man in the present, to
the understanding of redemption in Christ or to trinitarian
understanding. And in any case, too frequently such views take
short-cuts, failing to consider the full set of pre-conditions and
post-conditions for human existence.

V   The Relevance of Current Science

Where there are direct approaches to creation and eschatology
(as distinct from indirect), modern science is particularly
relevant as a major source for exact insight into the structural
constraints of existence. It is partly due to the widespread
avoidance of direct engagement with creation and eschatology
by theologians (as distinct from the indirect inquiries just
mentioned) that scientists and those of a speculative turn of
mind have turned to such wider issues. How far they are suited
to such tasks is another question. It seems that the approach
of scientists is necessarily limited; and they are confined to
limited, specialised studies. But not infrequently these are
collected and extended into more comprehensive restatements
of creation, and sometimes eschatology. These have not had
the careful critique which they need.

One of them merits brief consideration here, because of the
perspective it offers on the universe as a totality in time and
space, and the structure of space and time. Frank Tipler has
extended his earlier concerns with the anthropic principle to
study the future, simply because (as he says) it comprises
almost all of space and time – the next 100 billion years or so –
far more than the 20 billion years of its previous existence that
we can see. In doing so, he also seeks to rescue eschatology
from the hands of theologians who 'with a few exceptions . . .
are quite ignorant of [it]'.[14] His procedure is openly reductionist, translating all other concepts (including biology) into
the language of physics, regarding all forms of life as subject to
the same laws as electrons and atoms, and incorporating
theology into physics.

[13] Karl Rahner, 'The Hermeneutics of Eschatological Assertions', in *Theological
Investigations*, vol. 4 (London: Darton, Longman & Todd, 1966), pp. 330–1.
[14] Tipler, *The Physics of Immortality*, p. xiii.

His reasoned conclusion is that the Omega Point (his correlate for God) created the physical universe (and Himself/ Herself) in the sense that the latter emanated from the former; that much, he says, is quite consistent with physics. Tipler supports the theological meanings of creation: (1) that the physical universe has a finite age, that time itself had a beginning; and (2) that the universe is not self-sustaining, and could collapse into non-existence without the continuous act of God sustaining it. Furthermore, he says, the universe can and will eventually collapse as its temperature grows uniform; and yet we have the hope of 'resurrection', as all the information contained in our (and all historical) life is simulated in the mind of God. This is his integrated account of creation and eschatology.

Like this account or not, it is emblematic of what must be achieved in a direct approach to the task of providing a combined account of creation and eschatology, the successful integration of current understanding of cosmology (the structure and dynamics of the universe) with theology (an explanation of the normative conditions of the structure and dynamics of the universe grounded in a normative authority). If we wish to argue otherwise than does Tipler (or those whose arguments he uses), we must do so with the same comprehensiveness of argument.

Apart from those which arise both for God and creation from its emanationism, the chief fault of his argument is its poverty. Like many of the arguments which he uses, the synthesis which he weaves 'has something to say about everything, but does not tell us everything about anything' – or even enough about everything.[15] For example, while it maintains many convictions which theologians would want to maintain, it does so only by avoiding their full meaning.

There is no way to overcome such poverty except by reconsidering creation and eschatology in relation to God. It is to the task of outlining the lines on which such an account might proceed that we must now direct our attention. We shall approach the task from several directions. For reasons of clarity, I shall keep these separate from each other, arranging them in linked sections.

VI Creation and Eschatology, their Structures and Dynamics

First of all, let us make a preliminary statement about what creation and eschatology involve when seen in relation to each

[15] Martin Goldstein and Ilse F. Goldstein, *The Refrigerator and the Universe* (Cambridge, Mass.: Harvard University Press, 1994), p. 390.

other. On the one hand, creation constitutes foundational structures and dynamics which lead to, and delay, the end.[16] Hence, creation is itself infused with stability, that which is often implied by the use of the word 'nature', while also permeated by mobility, which is often implied by the word 'history': creation is thus 'nature' permeated by 'historicality'. On the other hand, eschatology introduces an irreducible tension as and in the very historicality of nature, whereby both nature and history are drawn to an as-yet-not-fully-specifiable realisation. This tension is intrinsic to them, and cannot be made extrinsic as a separable teleology; nature and history 'bear' this tension, as do the particulars and relations of which they are comprised.

The relation between creation and eschatology, put in the simplest terms, is this: in totality and in special aspects or regions, creation as constitution makes reference to the conditions of continuance and ending possible; it constitutes the universe in such a way as both to delay its ending, and to lead to its end. Eschatology, however, imparts an irreducible tension which is intrinsic to conditions, continuance and ending. The co-presence of the two marks all aspects of the universe as known in the past and likely to be known in the future. Comprised in this simple but general formulation, if fully specified, are those aspects of the universe which lend it stability and direction, and also those which provide it with mobility and energy;[17] but in all of them, as well as in their final outcome, there is a tension which directs it beyond itself.

That creation is that constitution of the universe which keeps it from ending, and brings it to its end, and that eschatology posits the tension which draws it to and beyond its end, apply differently for different elements and processes of the universe.[18] While the universe may last for 100 billion years, this earth will not; the earth will probably last longer than human beings; and so forth. In this, it is evident that creation gives them different 'capacities for finitude' according

---

[16] In other words, the world has an intrinsic structure and dynamics. This much can be said even where the exact nature of its dynamics – what kind of teleology is operative – remains in dispute.

[17] Hence, one might say, its 'conditions' are sensitive to 'special conditions' which make it turbulent and unpredictable in outcome. These interpenetrate each other to such a degree that there is neither order which is not to a degree chaotic, nor chaos which is not to a degree orderly.

[18] Whether the universe had a beginning as such, or will have an end as such, and if so what kind it was/will be, now much debated amongst scientists, should not halt the attempt to grasp the significance of the span from beginning (of whatever kind that might have been) to end (whatever that will be).

to their kinds and circumstances, and different possibilities for interacting with those other than themselves. In that sense, creation is a dynamic of particulars. While all begin and end in some way, there is a different time-span for each, which will vary according to the local provision of needs and the use made of its 'capacity for finitude'.[19] It is this which – variably – allows each both to be itself and also to be reliant on conditions beyond itself, while also making it sensitive to special conditions (and therefore turbulent and unpredictable in outcome). While these considerations are applicable to all elements of the world, they are especially important issues for all of the 'higher orders'.

At the same time, eschatology introduces for and in each (and all) a tension regarding its continuance and ending. The constitution of each particular – and the relations between them – is infused with historicality, understood not only as continuance but also as the coming of its ending. The coming of this ending, however, occurs as the decisiveness which marks each 'moment' of its existence and relations.[20] Hence, decisive 'turnings' are always being made by which particulars and relations are shaped, often irreversibly as one course is followed and others left.

> Two roads diverged in a wood, and I –
> I took the one less travelled by,
> And that has made all the difference.[21]

In such turnings, particulars or relations are shaped in such a way that the consequences are enduring for them even to the end. By whatever degree, they reconstitute the 'capacity for finitude' involved. And even at the end, the tension introduced by the *eschaton* allows for the transcending of the ending itself, in a fashion comparable to the transcending of beginning which is characteristic of creation's origin.

Taken in their interrelation, creation and eschatology therefore integrate space and time and the elements and processes by which they are mediated. As elements and processes, creation tells us the preconditions which are 'shaped' or 'completed' in the other; and eschatology tells us the range of possibilities – and then some – which are latent or manifest in the first, and in the beginning, but appear through the complexities and contingencies of history and its eventual transcendence. So, viewed ontologically, eschatology is the unfolding of what

---

[19] Hence it may be said that each is a spatio-temporal 'packet' which varies according to local circumstances and the use of the 'capacity for finitude'.

[20] This has been a consistent emphasis of the existentialists.

[21] Robert Frost, 'The Road Not Taken', in *Robert Frost: Selected Poems*, (Harmondsworth: Penguin, 1973), p. 78.

is enfolded in protology, but understood as a *novum* which appears at each point in the unfolding, even at the end.[22] It is not exhausted by what is provided in the constitution of creation. Creation itself is a transcendent constitution whose nature partially eludes those who are within the trajectory from creation to eschatology, and eschatology is a transcendent reopening whose character is similarly partially hidden. Nonetheless, the dynamics evident in the thrust of creation to eschatology provide our best window upon the two.

These considerations are much more profoundly important than appears at first sight. For what occurs in creation is spatio-temporal and material conditions without which there is no finite existence – without which there is nothing rather than something. Furthermore, what occurs is a certain order of spatio-temporality and materiality which allows for certain things to emerge – 'these' with their spatio-temporality and materiality rather than 'those'. And when things with certain spatio-temporalities and materialities come into existence, the structure and dynamics of creation keep them so, as more or less the same in the differences which appear through the dynamic temporal process of existence. 'For everything there is a season, and a time for every matter under heaven: a time to be born, and a time to die. . .'.[23] Speaking of us human beings, these structures and dynamics allot to each a time, keep us from dying and allow us to die – and along with us, others in the animate kingdom, eventually the world as we know it, and later (possibly) the universe. Existence only continues insofar as the structures and dynamics of creation operate to maintain it; and then it ends. But even during the course of existence, the historicality which is introduced by the *eschaton* brings many decisive turnings, as we have already seen. *Eschata*, and the transcending of the end itself which is implicit in them, happen when these structures and dynamics cease and are transformed.

From what source these derive, and how, we shall consider a little later. First, however, there is more to be said about the character of the structure and dynamics of the universe and its members.

VII Relations and Dynamics

If creation and eschatology considered together tell us about the spatio-temporality and materiality of the world, and the

---

[22] Cf. Jürgen Moltmann, *Religion, Revolution and the Future* (New York: Charles Scribner's Sons, 1969), p. 16.
[23] Ecclesiastes 3.1.

possibilities they have both for decisive shaping and re-shaping, they may also tell us the ways in which the varied spatio-temporalities of existent beings are configured with respect to each other – or how their varied 'capacities for finitude' are related. In other words, they may tell us how the universe is a spatio-temporal relational field. How are we to think of the varied othernesses and relationships which we find there? We cannot simply name them – 'othernesses' and 'relationships' – without seeking to explain how they are so.

As we saw, creation – both as a whole and in special aspects or regions – is that which keeps the universe from ending, and brings it to its end. Implied in this and the infusion of historicality and the *novum* by the eschaton, we found, were stability/direction and mobility/energy for existent entities. But these alone do not show how the world is a relational field, and a spatio-temporal one. How is it?

As we see the character of creation, it is clear that the varied spatio-temporalities of existent beings assign them varying stability and direction, and this constitutes their identities as different from each other, while their mobility and energy varyingly allow them to move freely as dissociated from others: they are themselves (identity) through dis-sociation (difference). There are a variety of relationalities in which such identity-through-dissociation may manifest itself, including at times using others as resources. But, at least in higher beings, the same features of their existence may also lead them to acknowledge comparable features in others, and make suitable allowance for them. In such cases, there is co-ordinate spatio-temporality, the basis of coexistence.

But a stronger relational field occurs where identity (stability and direction combined with mobility and energy) arises through the conferral of recognition and scope for positive freedom upon others as others. In such situations, the ultimate form is dedicated spatio-temporality, where identity is a consistent, directed choice of others and a movement toward them through which they are identified as themselves and honoured as such – to which they respond in trust. The theological term for such a dedicated spatio-temporality – by which there is identity through the con-ferral of otherness-in-honour – is election, and the result covenant. Although too frequently confused with contractual obligation, covenant – both as idea and practice – is the most advanced way of construing the dynamics of otherness in relationship. A more careful look at it is needed before we go on.

VIII   Conceptions of Covenant

Historically, the choice of Israel by the Lord God, and the covenant thus created between them, provided the primary vehicle for the understanding of themselves and others – and therefore of otherness and relations – throughout the history of Israel, and differently for the early Christians. Covenant was formative for their conception of others and the fulfilment of relations with them. Eventually, this choice and covenant was seen – as by Paul – to have been in Christ, in whose coming was made known the mystery of God's will (choice) as his plan for the fullness of time; this was the 'new' covenant, actually the recovery of the foundation and goal of the 'old'.[24] And the conception of how, as the people of Israel were chosen to be themselves yet in covenant with God, people themselves could be different from each other but 'one in Christ' and thereby different from and one with God, became a primary avenue for the enrichment of conceptions of otherness and relationship. This understanding permeated notions of difference and relation of all kinds: between people and the natural world, between people, and between them and God. The possibility of freedom was assured, but in and through that the possibility of well-being in relationships.[25]

There was also variation and development – although not irreversible progress – in the form of covenants. The earliest conceptions of covenants were largely obligatory, focused on the power of the originating party (e.g. in the early days seen as 'backed' by the gods as guarantors), with the emphasis on determination, regulation and obedience. The 'grace' with which such covenants were established was a form of power, and the determinations and obligations were inflexible. By contrast, in both the Sinaitic covenant, and much more emphatically in the promissory covenant of the Lord with Abraham and David, the 'grace' was a bestowal of freedom and benefits in return for trust and service; continued trust and service was expected, but the benefits did not cease if these were not as expected. A further development of the promissory covenant was, therefore, the inclusion of provision for alienation within the covenant designed to return the alienated to full standing, and thus construed as beneficial – a little like my daughter-in-law setting her child on the 'naughty step'. The covenant was not cut off, but construed more capaciously, as

---

[24] Ephesians 1.3f.

[25] This suggests that the otherness which is given is not formless but *shaped* in such a way as to provide the possibility – not the necessity – of well-being realised through life.

capable of including its negation – the possibility of disruption (e.g. of dynasty) and scattering (e.g. exile) – whose effects might be undone (e.g. forgiveness and restoration upon repentance). These were profound developments in the understanding of otherness in relationship. They clearly anticipated the other aspect of the 'new covenant' established in Jesus, where God – the same God whose choice and covenant and plan for Israel had occurred in Christ – was at one with the people not only in their otherness but also in their alienation. In their otherness and alienation, he was actively restoring relationships and justice.

The conception of otherness in relation could become very specific. One clear tendency was in the direction of ever more specific obligations expressed not as promises but as laws, laws governing the relations in the created order and between people which were seen as the 'law of God'. From this position, the history of covenant was retrospectively interpreted as the history of laws, which invited further legal refinement. This was a particular way of concretising the promissory conception of covenant, which had emphasised otherness itself and sociability through promises and reciprocal trust, with a minimum of institutions and formalised expressions. The main question was how these legal expressions were taken, whether as necessary for a more complex social situation (in latter-day Israel) or as sufficient for the highest kind of sociability.

Whatever the case, the distinctive character of the Christians lay elsewhere, in having found in Christ the mystery of the choice and plan of God, the basis for the constitution of creation and for the eschatological realisation of God's will. Hence, they had found the character of their otherness from each other and from God in the One who constituted (and reconstituted) their relation with God. But in due course, the Christians themselves tended to suppose that the necessary (laws) were sufficient for the relations of human beings to each other and to God. Both the Roman hierarchical social structure used in much church order, and also the Reformed/Puritan 'covenant of grace', have left lasting legacies of obsession with formal understanding in theology, social structure, law and legal protection.[26]

Notwithstanding this overspecification of the structure and dynamics of creation, both as idea and as practice, covenant is the most helpful way of construing the dynamics of the

[26] There appears to be a symbiotic relationship between such preoccupations with laws and the comparable obsessions of modern science with regularities.

establishment and maintenance of otherness in relationship, precisely because it recognises the possibility of otherness as gift, a gift which is enlarged by the well-being which may be achieved through the right use of otherness. It remains basic to theology and its contribution to human affairs. At the same time, its significance is by no means as fully recognised as might be expected, and discussions – particularly constructive ones – of the topic are relatively rare, in theology or elsewhere.

IX   Covenant, Creation and Eschatology

The importance of the conception of covenant for the present discussion is in its illumination of the structure and dynamics of creation–eschatology. That is, it elucidates not only the span comprised by creation and eschatology but also its provenance.

We have already seen that the very conception of covenant is rooted in 'dedicated spatio-temporality' – the positive conferral of otherness upon others for their fulfilment as such, to which the appropriate response is their movement toward this fulfilment. And this conferral has strong implications both for the one who confers and for those upon whom the conferral comes.

Looking first at those upon whom it comes, we can identify certain marks of this conferral. Speaking of the whole span of creation to eschaton, there is the simple fact of its otherness as given by the one who has conferred it, and the shaping thereby given it for its sustenance and fulfilment as such. And there is the positive thrust which always draws it beyond present conceptions of what these may be. In such fundamental characteristics, its provenance in the radical self-gift of God may be discerned.

In such ways, its otherness (from God) is determinative: it is not 'free-form' and shapeless, but has a determinative (as distinct from determined) shaping. Its marks as such are stability and mobility – stability as including a determinative shaping and the possibility of its own further self-shaping, and mobility as including a positive response to its situation in the world and to its future with that situation. Hence, the former is best seen as stable direction: it is causal but complex, and lends creation the equilibrium and unpredictability seen in the forms of existence in the world.[27] The latter is best seen as

---

[27] The ways in which it is so are not fully understood, and both different and more complex than formerly thought. One recent attempt to provide the new ontology which is required suggests an alternative approach to the very structure of evolutionary theory: 'That structure is *hierarchical*. Genes, organisms, demes, species, and monophyletic taxa form one nested

adaptive responsibility, the capacity to use energy for the benefit of the world – freedom in concrete responsibility as distinct from abstract freedom. Although the two interpenetrate each other, and cannot readily be separated, the former is formative, with constitutive constraints and limited latitude. The latter is transformative, comprised of the realisation of change and the conferral of benefit.

It is as well to remind ourselves that these marks are both ontological and moral: as such, they provide the conditions for existence and its ending, and also the possibility of creativity and change, including straying, redemption and return. The former is for existing. The latter is for qualitative development of all kinds, not least moral.

Both, however, are expressions of divine gift, a gift carried within the span formed by beginning, continuance and end, and discernible there as the structure and dynamics by which items are changingly the same as they are drawn toward their ending. As a whole and in the beings of which they are comprised, the determinative shaping and opening of the world, as well as their ending, are formed from the 'shaped space' constituted by divine gift and the response made by those who 'inhabit' it. They do not arise simply from divine determination and obedience, as for monarchical–legalist conceptions of divine creation.[28]

There is a danger, however, in seeing these characteristics simply as time-neutral fixtures. Every one of them is radically conditioned by the eschatological tension to which we referred earlier, 'drawn' through the tension by which the *eschaton* is pre-present. This too is carried within the temporal span formed in the continuance of the world. Exactly how it may be carried within creation is not fully understood. One possible explanation lies in the genetic constitution of organisms. For

---

hierarchical system of individuals that is concerned with the development, retention, and modification of *information* ensconced, at base, in the genome. But there is at the same time a parallel hierarchy of nested *ecological* individuals – proteins, organisms, populations, communities, and regional biotal systems, that reflects the *economic* organization and integration of living systems. The processes within each of these two process hierarchies, plus the interactions between the two hierarchies, seem to me to produce the events and patterns that we call evolution.' Niles Eldredge, *Unfinished Synthesis* (New York: Oxford University Press, 1985), p. 7.

[28] In this sense, the view presented here differs from the supposition that there is an *imago dei* in humanity which is determined by God to which human beings must be obedient. Humanity is constituted by the gift of difference (otherness) by God; and it is the fulfilment of this otherness, shaped in certain ways by God, to which human beings should aspire.

example, the genome project has shown that 90 per cent of a human's DNA is not part of any gene. It is apparently the sequences between genes that 'contain patches of DNA that control the use of the genes, and probably the ways in which associated sets of genes may be turned on or off in concert'. And long, 'pointless' stretches of repetition may be functional and –controlled by the structure of DNA – change over time, and tell the cells that time is passing.[29] Such 'timing', when taken with age-related changes in genetic configurations, may be one basic mechanism which 'carries' the coming of the end for that organism.

And it, as well as comparable features of the world, is an important aspect of the stable direction and adaptive responsibility of beings in the world, one which constantly requires their reconfiguration. Human beings are in a special position: within their limitations, they can with understanding and discipline respond – not simply to the 'carriers' of this eschatological tension but to the tension itself and its source in the gift of God. The value of human participation in creation-history is deeply dependent, therefore, on the quality of the human response both to creation and to the divine gift by which it is (will be) as it is (will be) – in all the ways through which humans affect the constitution of creation. The quality of this response rests on adequate appreciation of the 'shining mystery'[30] of the God whose own life is present in the gift of creation and humanity, order and freedom, who suffers to redeem it and us from the failure of our order, trust and community, and who imparts the energy for all otherness-in-relationships. This is the mystery of the character and life of the Trinitarian God.

X   The Radical Self-Gift of God

It is to the mystery of the activity of the Trinitarian God that we must now turn. What are the implications of the conferral of otherness on creation for the one who confers?

Let us look first at the act of conferral. As reflected in the shaping of the otherness which is conferred upon world-history, it appears that the conferral is an act which is definite, not formless or ambivalent. Insofar as the result is determinate in its possibilities for good, and not simply a confusion of alternatives, the conferral seems to be intrinsically good. This does not suggest a tightly-knit predetermination by which these

---

[29] See *The Economist*, 19 August 1995, p. 74.
[30] The term is chosen to convey the inexhaustible mystery which also constitutes itself as knowable.

good possibilities must be actualised, or that there is no scope for the non- or counter-realisation of these goods. The tension introduced by the eschatological opens good possibilities to their actualisation – or their negation.

What sort of conferral would constitute the world-history embraced by creation and eschatology as such? Should we expect an event of simple causation? Given the magnitude of complexity involved, that appears unlikely. The constitution of creation, and its permeation by eschatology, seem to be products of a certain kind of divine gift which constitutes the other as such and as deserving fulfilment in its own right. The divine act constitutes the other (universe, world, humanity and that of which each is formed) for fulfilment within its appropriate time-span.

A major problem for understanding this is that the divine act which constitutes the other for fulfilment is frequently presented in such a way as to be either less conceptually rich and interesting than, or to be incapable of explaining, the infrastructure and history of the universe, the world and humanity. This is the origin of the practical atheism which undermines so much theology.[31] Fundamental to the conception of the divine act of creation, therefore, is the existence of a creator from whose abundance the richness of creation as we know it originates and continues, and in which it ends – as distinct from (say) a bare causal principle which triggers, boosts or ends it.

Such a creator is one with a fullness of those characteristics which are imparted in the gift of otherness to creation, stable direction and adaptive responsibility, and those which are necessary to their sustenance. This implies that the creator is not an empty or formless infinite but one 'shaped' in a particular way, as unbounded, incomparably ordered and radically alive – the shaping of the trinitarian being of God. It is these 'perfections' which are found in the gift of the otherness, structure and dynamics of creation. Hence, this God is the complete source of all such things in creation's prevention and bringing of the end.

---

[31] This is closely related to the persistence of the monarchial conception of divine rule. Compare Hodgson's comment on Karl Barth: 'God rules creaturely occurrence by *ordering* it and thereby *controlling* and *directing* it. In agreement with the mainstream Catholic tradition against Calvin, Barth affirmed that creatures use their freedom under divine permission rather than compulsion, setting limits to it, and directing it to a common goal. This is accomplished by God's "ordering", "harmonising", and "coordinating" of the antitheses, conflicts and contradictions that are constitutive of world history.' Hodgson, *God in History*, p. 27.

Still more can be seen of this God if we see how creation is permeated by eschatology. Recognising that the otherness, stable direction and adaptive responsibility which mark creation are also mobilised by what we have called eschatological tension shows 'another side'. That this otherness is one drawn to fulfilment in its own sphere, that the stable direction is intended by God for the shaping of creation for its own good end, and that the adaptive responsibility of creation is mobilised for the fulfilment of the plan of God: these are the marks of the trinitarian presence of God in eschatology. They are strikingly akin to the covenant seen by Paul to have been in Christ:

> Although I am the very least of all the saints, this grace was given to me to bring to the Gentiles the news of the boundless riches of Christ, and to bring to light what is the plan of the mystery hidden for ages by God who created all things; so that through the church the wisdom of God in its rich variety might now be made known to the rulers and authorities in the heavenly places.[32]

In Christ, we know within God's gift of otherness that it is for fulfilment, the fulfilment of God's positive gift (that is, its stable direction) and that responsible performance (adaptive responsibility) will fulfil this plan. Both in creation and eschatology, the Trinitarian God is known through the activation and sustenance of the field spanned by creation and eschatology.

More needs to be said about the manner of the creative act of this Creator. It is the fullness of the Creator's gift of otherness which constitutes it as source for the otherness-to-fulfilment of creation. How is this so in the creative act? It is as stable and free to be fully and radically self-giving through acting to originate that which is other than God. It is this which gives rise to our notions of 'universe', 'world' and 'humanity'; they are neither self-generated nor human conceptual contrivances. Each has its wholeness and freedom contingently, and all of them in mutual relations, from the radical self-gift of God. That is, the nature, structure and history of the world and humanity are found not in their self-standing but in the radical – but contingent – gift of otherness-to-fulfilment by the Creator.

The nature of the origination which often dominates discussion of creation has to do with the radicality of these gifts by the Creator, not with conceptions of efficient causation no matter how powerful. Likewise, the notion of *creatio ex nihilo* (creation from nothing) derives from the denial of any source from which creation might have derived other than the

---

[32] Ephesians 3.10f.

Creator's existence, and the fullness of truth, goodness and beauty implicit in it. Both are expressions of the contingency of the field comprised by creation (that is, the universe, world and humanity) on the radical self-gift of the Creator.

A further challenge is to understand the implications for the structure and dynamics of the world. While it is important to stress the contingency of the world and humanity on the radical self-gift of God, such contingency must not be misunderstood. Being, truth, goodness and beauty are fully realised in God, and are as constant in the self-giving of God as they are in God; they are faithfully given to the world and humanity. It is this which confers upon both together (the relational field of world and humanity), as well as those which comprise each, an inalienable structure and dynamics – the stable direction and adaptive responsibility discussed earlier – proper to their existence together, beyond which they cannot go with impunity. Furthermore, the gift establishes the quality of this structure and dynamics for elements of the world and human beings separately and together: they are to be related as those who realise the being, truth, goodness and beauty in others through care and compassion, not through self-serving which makes others instrumental to inflated needs.

The purpose of the world is therefore to fulfil its finitude. It is important to recognise that in the constitution of creation, the fullness of the perfections of God, unity, truth, goodness and beauty, which are fully realised in God are not – and cannot be – completely given to finite beings, lest the finite be overcome by the infinite, 'become as gods'.[33] The radical self-giving of God is for the world and humanity to be themselves – and fully such; the perfections of God – pre-present to humanity from the *eschaton* – mobilise human beings to fulfil themselves. This movement to fullness forms the continuing course of the world and humanity, and forms the future whose arrival depends on the readiness of the recipient to move toward it. Their future is, in this sense, hidden in the eschatological self-gift of God.

XI   The Features of Creation

This awareness of creation provides it with some of its most remarkable features. The field of relations (in creation) which is the self-gift of God is a plenum, but one not fully realised. The first of these two features accounts for the seemingly infinite depth of the stable direction which we find in the

---

[33] Genesis 3.5

universe, world and humanity, that which inflames the passion of those who wish to find and know their fundamental character through time-neutral observation. The second of the two accounts for the indefinite dynamism of the universe, world and humanity in adaptive responsibility, in which they are seen as cosmically and historically open: they are always moving toward an as-yet incomplete goal, one which opens itself to them as they continue to understand and perform responsibly. The intersection between the two concerns and kinds of investigation – time-neutral and time-filled – is always a murky one, each always implying the other.

It was stressed earlier that God's self-gift is of the structure and dynamics comprised by the universe, the world and humanity. The same coupling of firmly given conditions with indefinite dynamism, is found in the field of relations within the universe, the world, humanity and God and between them. In that way, the radically loving self-gift of God not only establishes the boundaries of being, but 'shifts' them.[34] This suggests the remarkable fact that there is no fixed boundary either between God and creation, or within the creation: the very otherness between them may be a unity. God's self-gift not only originates that which is separate but constitutes a unity between God and the other which does not compromise the other's being in filling it. And it both invests the other with fixed obligations which are expressed as laws, and also indefinitely enlarges the possibilities of the other in its self-giving, as seen (for example) in qualities of compassion and care for others and the world. This is the nature of the ethical dynamism of creation.

As seen earlier, the personal character and freedom of the Creator arise from the Creator's fullness of existence, truth, goodness and beauty. We now see that these characteristics arise within the creation through the radical self-gift of the Creator, and are found throughout the field of relations in humanity and with the world. Precisely because this fullness of personhood and the freedom which flows from it are given to human beings, and to the world itself, however, there is the possibility of a radical misuse of the gift and its qualities (truth, goodness and beauty) by which they are alienated from their source (who is in turn treated as alienating) and taken as properties of the world and humanity. Even the constancy of

---

[34] The term is taken from a poem by Micheal O'Siadhail:

Gratuitous, beyond our fathom, both binding and freeing,
this love re-invades us, shifts the boundaries of our being.

'Out of the Blue' in *Hail! Madam Jazz* (Newcastle: Bloodaxe, 1992), p. 118.

the gift is taken over as these are considered intrinsic to those to whom God has given them. The result, evil in the case of the world and sin for humanity, radically dislocates all the relations proper to human beings in the world and fixes them within severely restricted conditions and purposes, structures and dynamics, thereby denying them both the true conditions of their being and the true future which they might otherwise anticipate. Such a dislocation can only be fully remedied by a decisive realignment of the 'boundaries' of and within creation, by a re-establishment of its structure and dynamics, of its stability and possibility. This is what occurs in the coming of the Redeemer, who confers new order and life in the presence of evil and sin.

XII   Creation and Eschatology Realised in Worship

Given this conception of the relation of creation and escha-tology to each other and to God, a large question remains. It is, in fact, the obverse of the covenant: if creation and eschatology are constituted by God's gift of shaped otherness, how do they most appropriately respond? More exactly, how are creation and eschatology to respond to the Trinitarian God in whose giving is their beginning, sustenance and end?

If the fundamental character of the trajectory of creation to *eschaton* results from an act of self-conferral by God by which it is formed in its otherness, the appropriate response would seem to be not only the fulfilment of the world in its otherness but also its fulfilment as explicit recognition of the gift of God. On the one hand, this would involve a dedicated use of spatio-temporality – and of the movement of creation to *eschaton* – for the sake of the world; on the other hand, it would embrace this movement – and its perfection – in dedication to God. The true character of the otherness of creation and eschatology from God would therefore be realised through relating them to their source in God. Such a relating could not be through acts extrinsic to them; it would require the activation of the movement from creation to *eschaton* as such (intrinsically, that is) in relation to God. A full relating of this kind is what occurs in worship.

To appreciate the significance of worship as the primary means of relating creation and eschatology to God, we must first understand its nature. In its primary sense, worship designates the response – acknowledgment in praise – evoked by the unfathomable depth of the giver of the gift of creation, whose unity, truth, goodness and beauty ('glory') are the source and end of all being, order and energy in existence. Although it is difficult for those habituated to human autonomy to grasp this, the response in worship is not self-generated but elicited by the quality of this glory – whose plenitude elevates all that responds to it in the fullest acknowledgment of which they are capable. In its secondary sense, worship is an encompassing activity in which all the dynamic of creation and eschatology is incorporated within the response made to that glory. In the one sense, worship is the intensive and engrossing manifestation of the plenitude of the self-giving God; in the other, it is the extensive and encompassing direction of all the universe, the world and human life toward that which has brought them to be and move toward their fulfilment.[35]

Like creation and eschatology, worship escapes the possibility of full or complete definition, for several reasons. Firstly, its concern with the fullness of the God whose being is hidden in the conferral of the otherness of creation makes it expansive and self-transforming, reaching always for the yet fuller being implied in the gift of otherness – beyond conceptions and practices based on lesser notions of the relation of God to the world, and lifting human faculties beyond confinement by such categories and forms. While it is not contentless or formless, this otherness-conferring plenitude always exceeds grasp by human conceptions and practices no matter how far their reach is extended.[36]

Secondly, at its profoundest level worship is both a synchronic and a diachronic activity, and thereby corresponds to the two aspects of the constitution of creation traced earlier, shaped direction and adaptive responsibility, and relates them explicitly to the plenitude of their conferral by God. In the one case, it is stimulated by intimations of the possibility of the

[35] The first sense follows the strict designation of the English term 'worship' (from the Old English *weorthscipe*, 'the condition [in a person] of deserving, or being held in, esteem or repute,' [*Oxford English Dictionary*]). The term signifies the having of worth or positive value, or the honour or dignity which is inherent in the one in whom it is found, and is therefore recognised by others. The second sense becomes more widespread in the humanistic climate which has prevailed since the European Renaissance, and is further accentuated in twentieth-century developments, where worship is often assimilated to the human task of constructing a full life. But more usually, worship incorporates the acknowledgement of a fullness of being, truth, goodness and beauty which is self-givingly constitutive for all else, and the responsibility of redirecting all else to the deepest possible relation to this plenitude.

[36] It is for this reason that worship is the principal means for rooting out idolatrous substitutes for God and for blocking magical attempts to dominate and manipulate it as these emerge within creation. The weakness of conceptions of worship today is correlative with the ready acceptance of forms of idolatry and magic.

ultimate unity and meaning of all things, and also by convictions of the presence of this unity and meaning for and in all things, its engagement with them and with us. In the other case, it finds such possibilities developed and confirmed through the ongoing rediscovery of their presence in the order of things and in history.

Thirdly, both aspects, synchronous and diachronous, are permeated by the eschatological, that eschatological tension discussed earlier.[37] Worship, particularly eucharistic worship, is intended to be a direct anticipation of the fullness of the *eschaton*, often through the enactment of present participation in the heavenly banquet. By these means, it concretises the anticipation of the *eschaton* and stimulates the movement by which creation as such is fulfilled for the sake of its giver.

Fourthly, worship – when fully practised – embraces all the features of life and understanding in the world and activates them in relation to their eventual goal. As such, it includes and activates all other forms of understanding and practice (such as the reason, understanding, ethical behaviour, and so forth) through enacting them in forms of prayer and symbolic ritual performances, of which more will be said below.[38] By placing these in the dynamic of worship they achieve their proper standing and empowerment.

Through these four movements, worship both identifies and activates the full dimensions of creation as constituted for its movement toward the *eschaton*, as these are carried by creation itself. But it also identifies and activates them in relation to their giver, as a fulfilment of the otherness given them. In worship, therefore, the Trinitarian God whose gift is present in them is found and responded-to. The self-giving of holiness which is comprised in the being and activity of the Trinitarian God in the gift of creation is recognised as constitutive of all the features of the cosmos, providing them with the fundamental orientation whereby they are freed for the fullest possibility which is theirs. It is within this recognition, concentrated in the dynamics of worship, that the development of human understanding of the 'nature' of the transcendent source occurs and continues.[39]

[37] This is seen in christological form in eucharistic rites: 'Christ has died. Christ is risen. Christ will come again.'

[38] Hence, for example, it can be said that preaching applies reason and moral understanding to life and understanding in the world and activates them in relation to their goal in God, while Baptism and Eucharist enact such life and understanding in symbolic ritual form.

[39] Such worship, and the understanding in which it results, embraces both mystery and illumination. In 'apophatic theology', as particularly emphasised in Eastern Christian thought, for example, it is only within a divine

XIII   Forms of Worship and their Place

The intensive and extensive aspects of worship are seen in its forms. Properly seen, these forms of worship may provide basic ways of activating the constitution of creation in its movement toward the eschaton. We must look at these forms before considering how they must be used if they are to do so.

They can be divided into two groups according to their use of spatio-temporality. Synchronous forms typically suspend spatio-temporal considerations, while diachronous forms incorporate spatio-temporal differentations.[40]

Synchronous forms are praise, confession, thanksgiving, inter-cession and petition.

(a) Because it is directed to the infinite plenitude of being, truth, goodness and beauty, worship is offered primarily as adoration and praise, expressions of gladness for the very being and self-gift of this God, in attitude and language refined to exalt God. It looks beyond creatureliness and creaturely thought to the very source of this plenitude, both unknowable in splendour (the apophatic element) and also self-conferring (the cataphatic element) in such a way that human beings can – at least provisionally – adore and praise him.

(b) The adoring and praising of God brings to light the shortcomings of those who do so. A second aspect is therefore the confession of the faults by which they have distorted their relation to God and those around them. For Christians, this is not simply an expression of penitence, but opening themselves to the goodness by which God overcomes these sins in Jesus Christ.

------

darkness like that which Moses entered on Sinai in meeting God, and through the purification of the senses, intellect and words, that God is found in a union of 'pure prayer' (Evagrius Ponticus, sixth century AD). 'Cataphatic theology', however, seeks to move toward God through the understanding of aspects of creation, while still recognising that God is beyond the very things – 'Being', 'the Good' and 'Life' – by which he is called through the use of notions from the created world. 'With these analogies we are raised upward toward the truth of the mind's vision, a truth which is simple and one. [Then] we leave behind us all our own notions. We call a halt to the activities of our minds and, to the extent that is proper, we approach the ray which transcends being' (Pseudo-Dionysius, sixth century AD). Both apophatic and cataphatic are ways of approaching God, in the one case through divine darkness and purification, and in the other through being raised upward through the mind's use of concepts from the created world. Contrasting emphases on mystery and illumination coexist in approaching the divine plenitude.

[40] This is to some extent a notional distinction, since each draws heavily on the other. We use it here for reasons of clarity.

(c) When the infinite plenitude of God is conferred upon human beings, and particularly in their salvation (cf. 'O come let us sing unto the Lord; let us heartily rejoice in the strength of our salvation', Psalm 95), the appropriate response (the third aspect) is thanksgiving. This is a responsive movement of the hearts of those touched by the movements of God toward them, by which they show gratitude for God's acts.

(d) It is equally important, however, that the world and these human beings be shaped through God's movements toward them. As regards 'the universe' in its various dimensions, God's actions are\ to be related to people and issues in the world through intercessory prayer, the fourth aspect. For Christians, this is a sharing in the work of Jesus Christ which holds together God and the world in his own suffering and dying, and a proclamation of God's infinite mercy as it is to be found everywhere. It is necessarily very specific, and requires involvement in the needs and pains of others. As regards those who worship, the movements of God's life are to be brought to bear on their lives – and all their details – in petition, the fifth aspect.

Diachronous forms operate somewhat differently, by sharpening, elevating and enriching the historical recognition of the nature of the plenitude whose movement toward human beings enables their adoration, praise, thanksgiving and petition. They involve the recalling (*anamnesis*) of the historical events by which divine plenitude has formed the basis of human well-being. The basis for worship is not (as Feuerbach thought) a metaphysical absolute which confines humankind in an alienated personification of himself ('God'), thereby dissipating his energies, but One whose history with humankind fulfils and energises it.

The two primary forms of diachronous worship for Christians are Baptism and the Eucharist. In each, all the elements of human understanding and life in the world are explicitly incorporated into the historical events by which creation is constituted and redemptively reconstituted.

As we have already noted, all of these forms of worship may provide fundamental ways of activating the constitution of creation in its movement toward the *eschaton*, thereby recognising the intrinsic relation between this movement and God's activity. Worship may incorporate all the features of life in the world and their movement to the *eschaton*, and also celebrate the activity of God which they carry. The reason it so frequently does not is probably that the forms of worship are laden so heavily with narratives of past situations as to lose touch with the task of activating present movement by reference to God's activity. That is, they concentrate so strongly on situations where God's actions and purposes were seen to have been intertwined with crucially important events, features and institutions of human life in the world, that the present purpose of worship is lost sight of.[41] A major recovery of the purpose of worship is needed if it is to recover its place in recognising and furthering the intrinsic connection between the movement of creation to *eschaton* and God's activity.

XIV Conclusion

We have explored creation and eschatology, the consequences of considering them together, the ways in which their relation derives from the gift of God, and the ways in which a response to God is appropriately made. This exploration has traversed many questions: how creation and eschatology are to be understood, their foundational structures and dynamics, the spatio-temporal relational field, dedicated spatio-temporality and the conception of covenant as the positive conferral of otherness for its fulfilment, the mystery of the Trinitarian God in whose

---

[41] Hence, for example, Hebrew worship concentrated on divine presence and action in the crucial constitutive events of and in time (creation, exodus and passover), the immediacies of human life (flesh and blood in the practice of sacrifice), social institutions (law and government), personal behaviour (offerings and hospitality), particular spatial locations (the land and shrines), specially-endowed representative personages (prophets, priests and kings), and so forth. The same features found in Hebrew worship are continued but radically transposed in Christianity, primarily through their comprehensive reshaping in relation to Jesus Christ. The very activity of God's blessing is seen to have occurred through God's relation with the world in Jesus Christ, through whom God chose his people even before creation – destining them to be holy and blameless, his sons in Christ, redeemed by his own blood from their trespasses to live in his grace and praise him. In effect, therefore, the fullness of worship occurs in Christ, and by being incorporated into Christ.

The implications of this transposition are extremely deep. The very plenitude of God is seen in a new light, as decisively turned toward humanity in history in the promise of the fullest blessing, whose form is covenant and redemption (of mankind from the sin which blinds them to God and distorts all existence). It is through the very movement of God's holiness toward mankind in the life, suffering, death and resurrection of Jesus Christ that mankind is purified and redeemed. Hence the very synchronic and diachronic character of worship is changed into 'remembering the Lord's death until he comes'. And finally, God is fully knotted together with humankind – in the Holy Spirit reordering and re-energising mankind for a new history with God, thereby conferring a new fullness of interactivity between human beings in their life together. All the ways in which the immediacies of life are incorporated in worship – institutions, rituals, personal behaviour, events of sacred history, and so forth – are transformed through being refocused on the fullness of God's work in Christ and the Holy Spirit, and given new norms. All of life is so intimately united to the life of Jesus Christ in the Holy Spirit that it serves to honour, adore and glorify the Father.

gift this occurs, the marks of this gift in the movement of creation to *eschaton*, and worship as an appropriate (but now problematic) way of recognising the intrinsic relation between creation, eschatology and the activity of God.

We must conclude, however, by recalling that it is, after all, the self-giving movement of God towards the other which is operative throughout creation and eschatology. And above all, it is the fullness of God from which this arises which requires recognition through the incorporation into worship of the movement of creation to *eschaton*. This does not violate the otherness which is established between them by the self-giving of God, but it does seek to maximise the relationship between them. By doing so, all creation and eschatology – that which keeps the universe from ending and that which ends it – is brought to glorify God. Creation and eschatology return glory to God – the very glory they are given through the trinitarian movement of God toward and in them.

> Then I saw a new heaven and a new earth; for the first heaven and the first earth had passed away, and the sea was no more. And I saw the holy city, new Jerusalem, coming down out of heaven from God, prepared as a bride for her husband; and I heard a great voice from the throne saying, 'Behold, the dwelling of God is with men. He will dwell with them, and they shall be his people, and God himself will be with them; he will wipe away every tear from their eyes, and death shall be no more, neither shall there be mourning nor crying nor pain any more, for the former things have passed away.'[42]

[42] Revelation 21.1–4.

7. Divine and Human Creativity

Brian Horne

Arthur Koestler's book *The Act of Creation*[1] immediately became the centre of public controversy when it was published: highly acclaimed by some, and severely criticised by others. It was momentarily famous, but it is not much read nowadays – forty years after its publication; perhaps because, as a philosophical study, it engages with issues that are not congenial to the fashions of contemporary academic philosophy or psychology in a language that is both idiosyncratic and yet highly dependent on the vocabulary of the experimental psychology of his own day. It would certainly not be found on the book lists of those involved in what is called 'critical theory' in the field of literature and the arts, despite the fact that Koestler's chief interest was the nature of the creation of the work of art. Denis Donoghue has recently remarked on the kind of attitudes that govern modern critical theory in the arts. 'If there is a single motive common to most of the ideologies, it is to deride any presumption of subject or self'.[2] *The Act of Creation* is too humane for such ideologies: at its centre is a fascination with the concept of personality, the human being as 'subject', the self as the originator and unique source of creative action.

For all its flaws it is not a book that can be ignored as it is still one of the few, sustained, systematic, modern attempts to describe and analyse the meaning and form of the human impulse to engage in an activity to which we give the name 'creation'; and while we may find the neologisms of Koestler's vocabulary quaint and the language of his experimental psychology dated, he, nonetheless, manages to throw a good deal of light upon a process that remains mysterious and controversial. It will be a useful starting-point in this attempt to understand the relationship between human and divine creativity.

---

[1] Arthur Koestler, *The Act of Creation* (London: Hutchinson, 1964).
[2] Denis Donoghue, *Times Literary Supplement*, 15 July 1994, p. 15.

The key-word of Koestler's argument appears quite early in the book. It is the word 'biosociative', and we shall find him arguing that all acts which can be described as creative display this feature: a connective and relational power that is peculiar to the human species. 'The biosociative act connects previously unconnected matrices of experience; it makes us "understand what it is to be awake, to be living on several planes at once" (to quote T. S. Eliot, somewhat out of context).'[3] It is part of Koestler's thesis that this phenomenon, the capacity to make something new, to bring about objects and situations that were not 'there' previously, by an act, at once intuitive and intellectual, of discovering the possibility of connecting hitherto disparate matrices of experience, is both distinctively and intrinsically human. It is *distinctively* human in that no other animal has this power: creativity is not a characteristic of nature as such but a property of human nature, it cannot be located in the realm of instinct. It is *intrinsically* human in that it cannot be regarded as the sole possession of those privileged members of the human species – Leonardo, Shakespeare, Mozart – to whom we give the name 'genius'. In the case of the genius, creativity is an intensification of a capacity inherent in the human race: the possibility of an act of creation lies within the grasp of all human beings to a greater or lesser degree.

The word 'biosociative' may be peculiar to Koestler but the concept of the creative act as a process of bringing together different matrices of experience is, of course, a much older theory, though it has seldom received so extensive a treatment as here in *The Act of Creation*. What is also of importance to his thesis is the belief that acts of creation are not confined to the world of art; humour and science are equally part of the creative impulse:

> When two independent matrices of perception reasoning interact with each other the result (as I hope to show) is either a *collision* ending in laughter, or their *fusion* in a new intellectual synthesis, or their *confrontation* in an aesthetic experience.[4]

It is extraordinary, and perhaps quite fortuitous, how closely the movement of Koestler's argument resembles that of Martin Buber whose stress on the essential relationality of all authentic experience is well-known. Writing at about the same time as Koestler he argued that we should see the creation of a work of art as a connective activity; an event of relation. 'It is

[3] Koestler, *The Act of Creation*, p. 45.
[4] Koestler, *The Act of Creation*, p. 45.

the work and witness of the relation between the *substantia humana* and the *substantia rerum*, it is the real of "the between" which has become form'; the act of creation is a 'relational event which takes place between two entities that have gone apart from one another'.[5] Of course there is a profound difference between the two approaches as well: the context and ultimate intention of Buber's thought gives his description of the creative act another and deeper significance. For if one reads Koestler with the aim of finding out *why* it is that human beings are creative one will be disappointed. This question launches us into the waters of metaphysical speculation that Koestler is not prepared to sail. However, there is a passage which tantalisingly points us in the direction of the kind of answer that might be given to this question: a passage which hints at a link between creativity and freedom (echoes of Buber's *substantia humana* and *substantia rerum*):

> There are two ways of escaping our more or less automatized routines of thinking and feeling. The first, of course, is the plunge into dreaming or dream-like states, when the codes of rational thinking are suspended. The other way is also an escape – from boredom, stagnation, intellectual predicaments, emotional frustration – but escape in the opposite direction; it is signalled by the spontaneous flash of insight which shows a familiar situation or event in a new light and elicits a new response from it.[6]

Biosociative acts (acts of creation) are seen as those acts which release us from the kind of determinism which is characteristic of the natural order, that is, of purely animal existence. To put a theological gloss on this we might say that in the non-human world (the natural order) creatures are simply what their appearance shows them as being: they are determined, without choice; they glorify God by being only themselves in their instinctive behaviour. In the human world it is different: there is freedom to choose, to act in certain ways which are willed and which may result in a creativity that will glorify God. But these are waters which, as I have said, Koestler refuses to set sail upon. These are the waters of metaphysics. Do we become free – and human – by acts of creation? Or do our acts of creation, our ability to bring about new and unexpected events and situations, arise out of our freedom? Is freedom the source or the consequence of our creativity? Koestler may avoid these questions but we may not, for they

---

[5] Martin Buber, *The Knowledge of Man. Selected Essays* (New York: Harper & Row, 1966), p. 66.

[6] Koestler, *The Act of Creation*, p. 45.

are fundamental to our understanding of the human person and, inevitably therefore, to our interpretation of the doctrine of the *imago dei*.

It is surprising, perhaps, when we look down the long history of Christian theology, that so few theologians have seriously and extensively addressed the question of human creativity or considered locating the meaning of the image of God in the power that human beings have of bringing into being 'secondary worlds' (to use the phrase of J. R. R. Tolkien). Perhaps its relative neglect is part of that phenomenon in the West in which the doctrine of creation has played a relatively minor role in the grand scheme of theological reflection. In much the same way as the doctrine of God the Creator has been seen as a necessary preliminary to the, apparently, more significant doctrines of God the Incarnate Redeemer, so the perception of man as the maker of things has provided merely the necessary material ground for what is more important: redemption and its associated doctrines of justification and sanctification. We shall not, after all, be making things in heaven, we shall be enjoying the beatific vision.

It is interesting to note that the *Oxford English Dictionary* can trace the word 'creativity' (in the sense in which we are accustomed to use it) no farther back than the late seventeenth century. The mediaeval Schoolmen, who were much more interested in art than is often supposed, placed art among the practical virtues. Those visionary, inspirational qualities which, since the early Romantic period, we have come to associate with the world of artistic imagination are virtually unknown to mediaeval thought – however visionary and inspired we in the twentieth century may find the sculptures of Chartres or the wall paintings of San Vitale. For the Schoolmen 'there are virtues of the mind whose *sole end* is *knowledge*. They belong to the *speculative* order ... Art, however, belongs to the practical order ... Its orientation is towards doing, not to the pure inwardness of being'.[7] Art is concerned with 'making'. We might call this 'craft'; and the Scholastic teaching comes as a surprise to a civilisation accustomed to thinking of art as 'expression'. Art as an exercise in self-expression; creativity as the impulse towards a material, sensuous formation of an inward personal vision is totally foreign to mediaeval sensibility and theory in which the creation of an artefact is 'useful': a productive action 'considered not in relation to the use to which

---

[7] Jacques Maritain, *Art and Scholasticism*, translated by J. F. Scanlan (London: Sheed & Ward, 1933), pp. 3–4.

we put our freedom but simply in relation to the perfection of the thing produced'.[8] Creativity as such, therefore, belongs in an order different from that of goodness or holiness; it is not part of the order of redemption. Nor was there any significant shifting away from this position for several hundred years following the era of the Schoolmen. I cannot think of a single Western theologian before the eighteenth century who might have constructed a theory of the image of God in terms of biosociative activity, that is, as something which lay in our capacity to act creatively; for the image lay in the sphere of being not in the sphere of doing; in what one was, not in what one did.

One can see how Scholasticism arrived at this conclusion. Since the time of Augustine, Western anthropology had turned inward to subjective experience to discover the truths about the nature of the human person in relation to God; and I see the *Confessions* as one of the foundation stones of the edifice that was erected. The concept of the mind became the dominating feature of Christian anthropology; and if one looked for the location of the image of God, one found it in the capacity to reason, not in the capacity to write poetry, build bridges, compose music or plumb palaces – except as all of these creative activities might be viewed as the happy result of the exercise of reason.

The Eastern theological and spiritual tradition presents us with a rather different picture and I shall refer to it later. First I should like to suggest that the very fact that our contemporaries are surprised and puzzled by the mediaeval attitude to art and creativity indicates the great change that has taken place in Western European sensibility – the reasons for which are complicated and which I have no time to discuss now. But along with the recovery (perhaps discovery) of the importance for theology of a doctrine of creation, so there has grown up, piecemeal and haphazard, an awareness that the classical approach to the understanding of the image of God is too limited and, even, misleading, and that the concept can be illuminated by the introduction of a theory of creativity. This has, occasionally, produced a theology which has affected not only our doctrine of man but our doctrine of God. So, for example, O. C. Quick in what was, in its time, an influential book, *Doctrines of the Creed*, examined the way in which an artist is involved with his or her work, loves it, delights in it, expresses himself or herself in it, and uses this picture of the artist as an analogy for God:

[8] Maritain, *Art and Scholasticism*, p. 7.

Since he creates out of the infinite resources of his own being, all things in various manners and degrees of perfection express him. It is thus that the artistic analogy leads us towards a conception of divine immanence which the analogy of the craftsman or machine-maker could not suggest.[9]

But I should like to consider the peculiar case of Dorothy L. Sayers in a famous book published only three years after *Doctrines of the Creed*, *The Mind of the Maker*.[10] It is an exposition of the doctrine of the Trinity and, at first sight, it is wholly Augustinian in its inspiration and ethos. What could be more like the arguments of *De Trinitate* than this use of the concept of the human mind as the model for the understanding of the life of the Divine? If, Augustine argues, we are made in the image of God, it is by the close examination of the workings of our minds that we shall arrive at true knowledge of their creator. The mind is tripartite, three and one at the same time, therefore God is both three and one. The corollary is also true: if God is revealed as Trinity then the mind of the being who is made in God's image must also be trinitarian in shape. But see what Dorothy L. Sayers does with this. She prefaces her work with two epigraphs, one of which is a quotation from Nicolai Berdyaev's book *The Destiny of Man*:

> In the case of man, that which he creates is more expressive than that which he begets. The image of the artist and the poet is imprinted more clearly on his works than on his children.

She is not, in fact, interested in Augustine's analogies and she quotes approvingly from Berdyaev again later: 'God created the world by imagination.'[11] We are a long way from Augustine and the Scholastic theologians here for whom the word 'imagination' would have had a quite different meaning – unthinkable in a theological context. But Sayers is using it in its modern sense and, moreover, making it the corner-stone of her own exposition:

> The components of the material world are fixed; those of the world of the imagination increase by a continuous and irreversible process, without any destruction . . . of what went before. This represents the nearest approach we experience to 'creation out of nothing' and we conceive the act of absolute creation as being an act analogous to that of the creative artist.[12]

[9] O. C. Quick, *Doctrines of the Creeds* (London: Nisbet, 1938), p. 45.
[10] Dorothy L. Sayers, *The Mind of the Maker* (London: Methuen, 1941).
[11] Sayers, *The Mind of the Maker*, p. 23.
[12] Sayers, *The Mind of the Maker*, p. 23.

There are echoes of O. C. Quick and, farther back, of George MacDonald's essay on the imagination written in 1867 – itself perhaps developing a theme which had already been powerfully set forth by S. T. Coleridge half a century earlier. This is the lineage of Sayers' theology. 'This experience', she writes, 'of the creative imagination in the common man or woman is the only thing we have to go upon in entertaining and formulating the concept of creation.'[13] This sounds like a very controversial and even foolhardy assertion indeed. The *only* thing we have to go upon? Is this analogy to be understood as the only analogy for absolute creation? Apparently not, for near the end of the book she remarks: 'For other minds, other analogies; but the artist's experience proves that the Trinitarian doctrine of Idea, Energy, Power is, quite literally, what it purports to be: a doctrine of the Creative Mind.'[14]

Like Augustine's *De Trinitate*, *The Mind of the Maker* is both a dazzling and a modest book. Her intentions are clear: she is attempting, like Augustine, to illuminate what has already been given in the tradition: the doctrine of God as Creator and the doctrine of God as Trinity. This is an explication of the self-revelation of God by way of a single analogy – and one that is of particular interest to us – the process of the creative mind. As I have already said, we will find the beginnings of this theology of the imagination already present in Coleridge, most particularly in the *Biographia Literaria*. Can we be satisfied with this theory of the relation between divine and human creativity? With Berdyaev's picture of God as the great Imaginer and ourselves, made in His image, as reflections of His imagination? The concept of freedom, mooted earlier, goes unnoticed in Sayers' exposition.

So far I have spoken only of the Western tradition; Berdyaev, however idiosyncratic he may have been, was nurtured in Eastern Orthodoxy, and it is in this tradition that the formulation of the idea of the *imago dei* in terms of creativity has been most vividly articulated. In his essay of the 1930s, 'Religion and Art', the Russian theologian Sergei Bulgakov, perhaps taking up themes that had already been played in Berdyaev's work of earlier decades, expounded the meaning of the thirty-first verse of the first chapter of *Genesis*: 'God saw everything that he had made: and, behold, it was very good.'

> God created man in his image, granting to this image three
> gifts: a mind directed towards the good, the gift of reason
> and wisdom, and the gift of aesthetic appreciation. Man is

[13] Sayers, *The Mind of the Maker*, p. 23.
[14] Sayers, *The Mind of the Maker*, p. 102.

meant to be the wisdom of the world, just because he participates in the Logos; he is also meant to be the artist of the world, because he can imbue it with beauty. Man must become not only a good and faithful worker in the world; he must not only 'dress and keep it' (Genesis 2.15), as he was commanded in Paradise, but he must become its artist; he must render it beautiful. Because he has been created in the image of God, he is called to create.[15]

This is a strong statement – 'meant to be', 'called to be', 'must' – and is in striking contrast to the tone and content of the British theology that approaches the subject from the same angle. There is no mention here of the word which is central to the thought of Coleridge, Newman, MacDonald, Sayers and many others: Imagination. But it is there in Berdyaev. Was this something he had drawn from his extensive contact with Western theology? Bulgakov uses a strange, and what might be considered a dubious, concept instead: 'Man has been called a demi-urge, not only to contemplate the beauty of the world, but also to express it.'[16] Leaving aside the propriety of the use of that word 'demi-urge' with its quasi-gnostic connotations, I should like to pause on the second half of that sentence: 'not only to contemplate the beauty of the world, but also to express it'. One need not be thrust into a gnostic mould for believing that this is true, and Bulgakov is at one with the other theologians I have mentioned in this interpretation of human creativity. It might be said, further, that in this perception the work of the artist does take on, perhaps surprisingly, the character of holiness. Far from being the result of an interior unique vision, that is, the self-expression of the artist, art has as its purpose the revelation of the beautiful already there but undiscovered in the world around us. (It is, interestingly a theory much closer to Koestler's biosociative understanding of creation: the connecting of hitherto disparate experiences which enables us to live on several planes at once.) Bulgakov continues:

Things are transfigured and made luminous by beauty; they become the revelation of their own abstract meaning. And this revelation through beauty of the things of the earth is the work of art. The world, as it has been given to us, has remained as it were covered by an outward shell through which art penetrates, as if foreseeing the coming transfiguration of the world.[17]

[15] Sergei Bulgakov, 'Religion and Art', *The Church of God. An Anglo-Russian Symposium*, edited by E. L. Mascall (London: SPCK, 1934), p. 175.
[16] Bulgakov, 'Religion and Art', p. 175.
[17] Bulgakov, 'Religion and Art', p. 175.

In this view human creativity as a process of self-realisation on the part of the artist which might or might not call forth a response from others – an important concept in Western aesthetics since the end of the eighteenth century – is set aside in favour of a capacity uniquely bestowed upon the human being for discovering and presenting in signs – shapes, colours, sounds, and so forth – the true nature of reality, a nature which is usually obscured, hidden or distorted. What is unclear in Bulgakov's writing is whether this reality is hidden and obscured as the result of sin or whether, in a semi-Platonic manner, the material world itself obscures the beauty of purely spiritual reality. Is art the restoration of pristine glory corrupted by Original Sin or the presentation of a glory beyond the confines of the material order? Much of Orthodox writing in the field of aesthetics leaves this unclear.

A similar approach and ambivalence may, for example, be observed in Philip Sherrard's attempt to address the question of human and divine creativity in his book.[18] A central place is given to a chapter on the art of the icon:

> The icon is not an imitation of the natural world, . . . it does not enter into competition with the unattainable perfection of the world, as the classical art, for instance, so often tries to do; nor does it aspire, again as classical art so often does, to a serenity in terms of this world – an aspiration which, because of its impossibility, results in a falsifying idealism . . . it seeks to convey to us a picture of the divine world order – that is, a picture of how things are in their true states, or in the eyes of God; and not as they appear to us from our limited point of view.[19]

As in Bulgakov's writings, this capacity to create is crucial for Sherrard's doctrine of the *imago dei*: it is not the whole of the *imago dei*, but it is central: '. . . by virtue of the fact that man is created in the image of God, he is also a creator, a maker, an artist. Indeed this is his distinguishing role, that which is capable of making him holy'.[20] Not only do we notice the conjunction of creativity and holiness, but we notice how divergent this is from the tendency of the Western tradition. The mediaeval theologians, with their clear distinction between the speculative and the practical orders, would have seen nothing holy about the making of things: holiness lay in the sphere of being rather than that of doing: it was a matter of moral virtue

---

[18] Philip Sherrard, *Sacred and Profane Beauty* (London: Golganooza Press, 1993).

[19] Sherrard, *Sacred and Profane Beauty*, pp. 74f.

[20] Bulgakov, 'Religion and Art', p. 175.

not a question of skill of hand or eye. Further, until recently, the Western tradition seldom used the vocabulary of 'transfiguration' in connection with art, whereas Berdyaev, Bulgakov and others make a point of saying that the artist's function is to contribute to the transformation of the world as it now is into the world as it should be. This is profoundly eschatological. However, Western theology is not without witnesses here, and Sherrard quotes a passage from Etienne Gilson's book, *The Arts of the Beautiful* (perhaps influenced by Berdyaev) in which the eschatological note is clearly sounded: 'Thanks to the fine arts, matter enters by participation into the state of glory promised to it by theologians at the end of time, when it will be thoroughly spiritualized.'[21]

Is this where our journey ends? Arthur Koestler suggested that the act of creation was a kind of biological necessity: we are what we are (creators) because this is where the process of evolution has brought us. We, by contrast, have arrived at a position of seeing the act of creation as a theological necessity: we are what we are (creators) because we have been made in the image of God. Can we be satisfied with this as an explanation of the relation between human and divine creativity and leave it at that? Only up to a point, for there is still too much unexplained; and, to be fair to most of the theologians I have been quoting, they have also realised this to a greater or lesser degree. We have to turn our attention again to what it is we create if we want to see the complexity of our search; a complexity which involves the questions of the relation of a work of art to a world broken by sin and the operation of freedom in that world.

Even if one were to grant that the bringing into being of a work of art is not adequately defined merely in terms of the realisation of a subjective, personal vision of reality; even if one were to grant the probability of human creativity possessing a revelatory, even transfiguring power, the process of the production depends not only upon the technical skill of the artist or craftsman but upon the interior, and to that extent private and unique, vision of the man or woman who fashioned the elements of the material world into sensuous forms. And that interior vision will have been shaped by the thousands of pressures and influences, mental and physical, that constitute the cultural context of the artist. Unless one were to restrict the category of art solely to the creation of the icon, a process in which the personal vision and will of the painter is, by prayer and discipline, conformed to the mind of Christ, one would have

[21] Sherrard, *Sacred and Profane Beauty*, p. 151.

to admit that our explanation so far is too simplistic and too limited. We cannot consign all art that is not specifically created to embody the tradition of the church to the realm of non-art; and Philip Sherrard is well aware of this. He knows that it would be ludicrous to deny that a human creative genius is operating in works which make no reference to the divine, and even those works which, in words or images, transfigure the world horribly into pictures of terror and despair rather than into representations of joy and glory. He mentions 'The Waste Land' by T. S. Eliot as a specific instance of such dreadful transfiguration: I would mention the opera *Wozzeck* by Alban Berg. There are thousands of others.

What all creative efforts represent is not simply a biosociative activity, though that description is useful as far as it goes, nor even an attempt at signifying an ideal pattern of reality, that is too restrictive. What they share is a wrestling with intractable existence: an effort at drawing meaning out of inert nature. This does not imply that the non-human world is, of itself, without meaning, but our relationship to it is problematical and our attempts at artistic expression are attempts at comprehending the possibilities of a relationship that is unproblematical. Paul Tillich succinctly summarises this in a passage in his essay 'Art and Society':

> Art does three things: it expresses, it transforms, it antici-
> pates. It expresses man's fear of the reality he discovers. It
> transforms ordinary reality in order to give the power of
> expressing something which is not itself. It anticipates possi-
> bilities of being which transcend the given possibilities.[22]

Somewhere along this trajectory all works of art will find their place. Some will be at the beginning, expressions of the fear of the reality we discover: the determinism of nature, death, and the inescapable pains and horrors of a world disordered by sin. Some will be located in the middle – examples of the artist's power to awaken us to possibilities that had not been noticed before. Others will lift us beyond what and where we are into a world which can be known only in anticipation; art whose images are imbued with ecstasy or eschatological hope.

But they all arise out of our freedom; and with this I return to the question I raised some time ago: the relation between freedom and creativity. I have no hesitation in asserting that we are creators because we are created in the image of God the Creator. At the same time I shall assert that there is an ontological difference between our capacity to create and the creative activity of God. This is where paradox arises. Our

[22] Paul Tillich, *On Art and Architecture* (New York: Crossroad, 1989), p. 18.

freedom is peculiar to our natures as creatures, it is not the
absolute freedom of the Divine. It would appear that just as
we are free to love or not to love, so we are free to create or not
to create. But freedom is freedom *for* something, not merely
freedom from something. It is not a quality which can exist, as
it were, in potential. So creativity cannot exist in potential,
just as love cannot remain unexpressed. We are not free *not*
to create. So, having stated that our creativity arises out of
our status as free creatures, I must also say immediately
that unless we create we lose that freedom and fall away,
existentially, from the *imago dei*. This is where a clear distinction can be drawn between divine creativity and human
creativity; between God himself and the image of God in us
his human creatures. The creation of the world and the
building of Grand Central station both arise out of freedom,
but arise quite differently. The creation of the world is the
act of absolute freedom; it comes into being out of nothing; it
is not the re-ordering of pre-existent matter; it is not God
wrestling meaning out of recalcitrant nature. There are no
constraints upon this act; God expresses nothing but himself,
for there is nothing else to express. That human beings are
able to plan and execute something like Grand Central station
or the Brancacci frescoes also arises out of freedom, but
freedom that can only be understood in relation to necessity.
On the one hand nothing compelled human beings to erect
Grand Central station or the Brancacci frescoes as such – they
are not part of the natural order; on the other hand some such
artefacts must be constructed if our freedom from the
determinism of the natural order is to be achieved. Here we
see the importance of stressing what at first sight seems so
obvious a proposition that it appears banal to state it: that
we cannot, in the strict sense, create anything out of nothing.
The inability to bring into being, in the sheer physical sense,
what was not there before is the measure of our con-
strainedness: the ability so to re-order the matter of our
universe into shapes, patterns, colours, sounds that are
totally new is the measure of our freedom. To quote Paul
Tillich again: 'Man stands between the finite he is and the
infinite to which he belongs and from which he is excluded.
So he creates symbols of his infinity.'[23] What is created is not
being itself, but symbols of being, or rather signs of new
being. Berdyaev again, in *The Beginning and the End*, sees
creative activity (not only in the fine arts) as a power 'to
carry on the creation of the world and anticipate its trans-

[23] Tillich, *On Art and Architecture*, p. 17.

figuration'.[24] We are not compelled to re-order our world and our experience of the world, but if we do not engage with the world and our experience of the world in the form of creative acts we submit to our existence in the world in all its determinations. The *possibility* of creation is lodged within the existence in mankind of the image of God; the *necessity* of creation is lodged in our creatureliness as part of the determined material universe. We live out our lives in the tension between freedom and necessity; and human creativity can only be properly understood in this context. Like God we are able to exercise our freedom in the creative act; unlike God the creative act is one of the necessary ways in which that freedom is realised.

[24] Quoted by Fuad Nacho, *Berdyaev's Philosophy* (London: Victor Gollancz, 1967), p. 10.

8. God, Creation and the Christian Community: The Dogmatic Basis of a Christian Ethic of Createdness

Christoph Schwöbel

I Faith and Action – Dogmatics and Ethics

In recent years we have experienced a remarkable rearrangement of the theological agenda. The topic of creation which, for almost two hundred years, had played a subordinate or, at least, contentious and highly problematical role in systematic theology has received a prominent place as a major focus of theological attention – in churches, universities and at theological conferences. In many of its aspects this development reflects the way in which Christian theology is and always has been bound up with the spirit of the times, the needs and questions of the cultural situation. The world-wide ecological crisis has for all of us challenged our ways of thinking about the world we live in and our ways of acting in this world. It is only appropriate that Christian theology should address this challenge. Since the Christian gospel claims to be valid for all situations and for the spirit of all times, it should also have something to say in our situation and to the spirit of our times, characterised as they are by the awareness of the ecological crisis. Theology's desire to be relevant is an implication of the character of the Christian gospel which sets the task for Christian theology.

However, it is a point of historical experience that whenever Christian theology has attempted to be relevant and, more so, to prove its relevance and has thus engaged in apologetics, it has tended to become entangled in the tension between demonstrating its relevance and maintaining its identity, or it has been in danger of creating antinomies between the implications drawn from the gospel and the content of the gospel itself. It is perhaps not an exaggeration to say that every movement later deemed heretical has at its core a genuine concern for relevance which is to be treated with utter seriousness. Conversely, the effort to define or to restore orthodoxy has often consisted in clarifying the relationship between implications drawn from the gospel and the central contents of the gospel itself and so to recover its identity.

Some of the responses of some Christian theologians to the environmental crisis seem to point to difficulties of this kind. One example may suffice. Many of the reactions of theologians to the environmental crisis focus, quite correctly, on an ethical response to the situation.[1] Since we are responsible for threatening far-reaching destruction to creation it is argued that it is now our responsibility to preserve creation from destruction. A theological ethics of creation is therefore called for as a guide for translating this ecological imperative into concrete action. However, with this line of reasoning a number of important theological distinctions are in danger of being blurred. Inflicting destructive effects upon creation falls indeed within the realm of human responsibility and has therefore from the earliest times onwards been interpreted as sin: bringing destruction to creation means offending its Creator. Yet, the preservation or restoration of creation cannot be a human task if this creation is continuously created and preserved by God who brought it into being in the first place. Theologically, creation, including the sustaining and preserving of creation, is a divine and not a human work. Therefore, creation is not in the same sense a field of human action as, for instance, politics, science or business. While it is proper, and indeed necessary, to speak of the ethics of politics, of science or of business ethics, the term ethics of creation contains a dangerous ambiguity. It seems that the same absolutism of human action which has characterised the human exploitation of creation is now returning in the guise of rescuing it. The search for relevance, so it appears, comes into conflict with fundamental dogmatic tenets of a Christian theology of creation. What seems to be needed is not an ethics of creation, but an *ethic of createdness* which is informed by a *theology of creation*.[2] The question of the relationship between a Christian ethics of createdness and a Christian theology of creation therefore seems to be an

---

[1] A survey of the relevant literature can be found in two review articles by Christofer Frey: 'Theologie und Ethik der Schöpfung', *Zeitschrift für Evangelische Ethik* 32 (1988), pp. 47–62, and 'Literaturbericht: Neue Gesichtspunkte zur Schöpfungstheologie und Schöpfungsethik', *Zeitschrift für Evangelische Ethik* 33 (1989), pp. 217–32.

[2] I have argued for this task in my article 'Theologie der Schöpfung im Dialog zwischen Naturwissenschaft und Dogmatik', *Unsere Welt – Gottes Schöpfung. Festschrift für Eberhard Wölfel* (Marburg: N. G. Elwert, 1992), pp. 199–221.

illuminating test-case for the general issue of the relationship between dogmatics and ethics.

Christian faith and Christian action form an indissoluble unity. There is no faith that does not generate a specific form of action, otherwise we would call the presence or the authenticity of faith into question. And there is no action that does not presuppose some sort of faith, otherwise we would feel justified asking whether such behaviour could qualify as action. In fact, we see it as a legitimate and productive criterion to assess the character of faith by the fruits it produces, since faith is a constitutive element of a person's capacity to act. Action not only presupposes certain beliefs about the subjective and objective possibilities of action, about aims and norms of action. It also presupposes faith as fundamental trust in the veracity and value of these beliefs that enables us to take positive action. Faith without action is empty, action without faith is blind.

However, in Christian faith and action this unity is specifically structured. Faith is not the product of human action, but the product of divine action, the work of God the Spirit authenticating the gospel of Christ to us as the truth about our created destiny to live by grace as the daughters and sons of God the Father. Although the constitution of faith is God's work and faith is therefore passively constituted for us, the life of faith is the human activity of recognising and appropriating this divine work as the fundamental orientation for all our actions. Luther who more than any other theologian insisted that faith is not a product of human action[3] could therefore characterise faith as *the* human work, the fundamental act of Christian faith.[4] As existential trust in God, Father, Son and

---

[3] Luther, on the one hand, frequently characterises faith as God's work in us which completely transforms us and gives us new birth. One of the classical passages is the following from the Preface to the Epistle to the Romans where the works of the law and faith are contrasted: 'Des Gesetzes werck ist alles, das der mensch thut oder thun kan am Gersetze aus seinem freien willen und eigen krefften. ... Aber Glaube ist ein göttlich werck in uns, das uns wandelt und new gebirt aus Gott, Johan. 1. Und tödtet den alten Adam, machet uns gantz ander Menschen von hertzen, mut, sinn und allen kreften ...' (WA DB 7, 6, 2f. and 11, 6–8).

[4] Luther could, on the other hand, characterise faith as the first and foremost, the noblest good work, perhaps in its most impressive form in the Sermon 'On Good Works' from 1520: 'Das erste und hochste, aller edlist gut werck ist der glaube in Christum ... , denn mit keinem andern Werk mag man Gott erlangen oder verlieren, denn allein mit Glauben oder Unglauben, mit Vertrauen oder zweifel; der andern Werke reicht keines bis zu Gott' (WA 6 204, 25f. and 217, 34–36). What seems at first a clear contradiction or, because of the numerous passages that could be adduced for both statements, a systematic ambiguity, can be shown to be a clearly defined relationship

Spirit, faith defines the fundamental direction of all our activity, both of our symbolising activity, finding expression in language and beliefs, and of our organising activity, finding expression in our actions. The fundamental content of faith is what God gives to us in the threefold divine self-giving as Father, Son and Spirit in order that we should be enabled to do God's will in all our actions. Without faith God's commandments confront us with our inability to act in accordance with God's will; through faith doing God's will becomes the new obedience in which Christian faith takes shape in the Christian life. Faith is thus the primary instance of what createdness means. With regard to its constitution faith is *creatura verbi divini*, the creature of the divine word, with regard to its practice it is the *character creaturae humanae*, the defining characteristic of the human creature.

Because the unity of Christian faith and Christian life is structured in this particular way, the difference between dogmatics and ethics is primarily one of *method*. While the primary task of dogmatics is to offer an argued and coherent exposition of the content of Christian faith, a conceptual reconstruction of the discourse of Christian faith, it remains incomplete unless it can demonstrate the ethical implications of the Christian understanding of reality it seeks to develop. Every dogmatic *locus* has an ethical point, an ethical *Sitz im Leben*, since the faith it explicates is the fundamental orientation of the Christian life. Conversely, while it is the primary task of Christian ethics to offer a description of the ethical goods, virtues and duties characterising the Christian faith, a conceptual reconstruction of the criteria and forms of action of the Christian life, it remains incomplete unless it can indicate the dogmatic presuppositions and implications of the Christian policy of action it seeks to develop. Every ethical concept has dogmatic presuppositions, it has a dogmatic *Sitz im Glauben*, since the life it describes rests on the fundamental orientation of Christian faith. It is for this reason that the difference between dogmatics and ethics concerns the method, the perspective and procedure of exposition, and not the

---

between statements referring to the *constitution of faith* as God's work and the *practice of faith* as a human activity. The distinction and relation between both becomes clear, if we understand the constitution of faith as the reconstitution of the human capacity for action which is lost under the rule of sin, and the practice of faith as the obedient human response to this divine work. A comprehensive analysis of the understanding of faith as a divine and/or a human work can be found in Wilfried Härle's study 'Der Glaube als Gottes- und/oder Menschenwerk in der Theologie Martin Luthers', in *Glaube. Marburger Jahrbuch Theologie* IV, 1992 (Marburg: N. G. Elwert), pp. 37–77.

content.[5] Both have as their theme the distinction and the relation of divine and human action which is the fundamental and distinctive theme of all Christian theology, because it is a fundamental requirement of the Christian life.[6] I will now attempt to sketch the dogmatic bases of a Christian ethic of createdness, always keeping in mind that it would be just as possible and legitimate to set out the ethical foundations of a Christian doctrine of creation, provided this attempt is undertaken as the description of the Christian life which is anchored in faith as the creature of the divine word, the exemplary case of createdness.

II   God the Triune Creator

The dogmatics of Christian faith, the statements expressing the truth-claims asserted, presupposed and implied in the practice of Christian faith, form a complex whole, a network of relationships in which one set of statements supports and is supported by other statements. Observing these interconnections and trying to determine their character and logical form

[5] This view of the relationship between dogmatics and ethics differs both from Wolfhart Pannenberg's and from Karl Barth's. Pannenberg has argued (against Barth) that the distinction between dogmatics and ethics is not simply a division of labour but is a material distinction: Ethics addresses humans as agents while dogmatics focuses upon God and God's action (cf. *Systematic Theology*, vol. I, Edinburgh: T. & T. Clark, 1992, p. 59 n. 128). This division runs the risk of undercutting the dogmatic foundations of ethics and of depriving dogmatics of its ethical point. This can only be avoided if the distinction and relationship between *opus Dei* and *opus hominum* is the common theme of dogmatics *and* ethics which are not distinguished by their content, but by the method employed in each field. However, Barth has criticised attempts to distinguish dogmatics and ethics with regard to method as problematical, since this – he claims – regularly leads to an impossible shift of perspective and to a fatal exchange of subjects (i.e. of God and humanity) which then becomes the constitutive principle of ethics. He suspects that such a distinction would make human works and words central for ethics at the expense of the divine Word and works (cf. *Kirchliche Dogmatik* 1/2 (Zürich: Theologischer Verlag Zürich, [6]1975), p. 884). This criticism loses its point if we see the distinction and relationship between divine and human action as it is exemplified in Christian faith as the common theme of dogmatics and ethics. If God's action in constituting faith is the constitution of the human capacity for action, it becomes theologically impossible to talk of human subjects of action apart from their constitution through God's action. By viewing the relationship between divine and human action as the common content of dogmatics and ethics which are distinguished by their methods, we can try to avoid the pitfalls of views which see *either* God and divine action *or* humanity and human action as the subject-matter of ethics and/or dogmatics.

[6] This, at least, was Luther's view: '*Oportet igitur certissimam distinctionem habere inter virtutem Dei et nostram, inter opus Dei et nostrum, si volumus pie vivere*' (WA 18, 614).

therefore often provides essential clues for understanding a specific set of doctrinal statements. A major feature of doctrinal history consists in describing and analysing how specific statements concerning one set of statements occasioned parallel developments in other spheres of dogmatic expression. The doctrine of creation provides a good example for this interrelationship. It developed in relation to other developments in christology, soteriology and especially in relation to the deeper apprehension of the identity and nature of God. The question 'What does it mean to say that God is the Creator?' could not be answered without simultaneously attending to the question 'Who is this God of whom we confess that he is the Creator?' Questions and answers concerning the identity and nature of God provoked and responded to other questions and answers concerning the agency of this God, not least in creation.[7]

This interrelatedness is also reflected in the mixed and overlapping forms of reasoning employed in Christian dogmatics. Philosophical reasoning and conceptual arguments are combined with scriptural references and interpretations in such a way that the scriptural witness provides the occasion for philosophical reasoning and the context of conceptual reflection. What is particularly interesting is that the question 'Who is this God of whom we confess that he is the Creator?' is, of necessity, answered by referring to scripture. Identity questions must be answered by narratives, by telling a story that provides an identity description. In trying to say who it is whom Christians confess as the Creator, Christians have always had to tell the story of God's relationship with Israel, of God's presence in Jesus and his presence for the church and the world in the Spirit. The identity of God provides in Christian dogmatics the basis for questions about the character of this God and the nature of God's relationship to what is not God. In thinking about God the Creator Christians have always felt it necessary to relate this to the other things they have said about God. Talking about the Creator implies the task of relating this to statements about God reconciling the world and about the hope of God bringing about the perfection of the relationship with creation. The context of such discourse is the way in which Christians believe that they experience the present reality and hope for the future consummation of what is promised in scripture. Scriptural references to God

---

[7] Cf. on the relationship between 'who?'-questions and 'what?'-questions the illuminating account of R. W. Jenson in the second locus 'The Triune God', in C. E. Braaten and R. W. Jenson (eds), *Christian Dogmatics* (Philadelphia: Fortress Press, 1984), vol. 1, pp. 79–191, especially 79–86.

reconciling the world have their particular weight in that Christians believe that they experience what scripture talks about as the foundation and reality of the life of the Christian community. The experience of faith of the Christian community which is documented in a particular way of relating and being related to the witness of scripture is therefore a constitutive aspect of the way questions about God the Creator are dealt with in Christian dogmatics.

It is against this background that it can be claimed that the doctrine of the Trinity is the summary expression of what Christians have to say in answer to the question who God is and what God is in the divine life and in relation to what is not God.[8] The Christian answer to the question 'Who is God?' is: the Father, the Son and the Spirit. The invocation of the threefold divine name is the only appropriate response to the self-identification of the God of Israel in Jesus Christ through the Spirit. This is the result of the hazardous and often contentious process of attempting to grasp the truth of God's self-communication witnessed by scripture that comes to a preliminary conclusion in the ecumenical councils of the fourth century.[9] As the summary expression of what Christians have to say about the identity of their God, the doctrine of the Trinity brackets what they say about the character of this God and relates what they say about God creating, reconciling and perfecting the world. Christians conceive the unity of divine action in seeing this unity mediated through the unity-in-difference of the personal communion of Father, Son and Spirit. Therefore the doctrine of the Trinity provides the framework that regulates the interplay between Who?-questions and What?-questions in Christian theology, between scriptural interpretation, conceptual reflection and reference to the experience of the Christian community. If this is true, then the decisive question for dogmatic statements about God the Creator concerns their relationship to statements about the Trinity. In what sense can we speak about God the triune Creator and what difference does it make to our understanding of what it means to confess God as the Creator of heaven and earth? What can be gained by understanding the triune God as the Creator? Three points can be made here.

[8] Nicholas Lash calls the doctrine of the Trinity "'the summary grammar" of the Christian account of the mystery of salvation and creation'. 'Considering the Trinity', *Modern Theology* 2 (1986), p. 183.
[9] Cf. the discussion of the nature of this process in R. P. C. Hanson, *The Search for the Christian Doctrine of God* (Edinburgh: T. & T. Clark, 1988), pp. 869–75 with the alternative account in Thomas F. Torrance, *The Trinitarian Faith. The Evangelical Theology of the Ancient Catholic Church* (Edinburgh: T. & T. Clark, 1988).

1. The doctrine of the Trinity helps to secure the distinction between creation and the Creator by contrasting the relationship of God to the world with the inner-trinitarian relations. According to the Christian understanding of creation, the world is the result of God's free and sovereign action.[10] It is therefore neither necessary nor eternal. Classically appeal to the Trinity is made in order to secure this distinction between the Creator and creation. If the world were eternal it would be the Son who is the eternal correlate of the being of the Father.[11] The *homoousios* of trinitarian theology depicting the relationship of Father and Son as one of ontological coequality here plays a critical role in determining the ontological status of the world as one of contingent, that is created, being.[12] This can be brought out by contrasting the relationship in which God stands to the world that is *created* with the relationship between the Father and the Son who is *generated*. In this way two relationships are distinguished: the relationship between the Father and the Son which is constitutive for the divine being – without the Son there could be no Father, without the Father no Son – and the relationship of God to creation which is not constitutive for the being of God but the result of a free act. The contrast of these relationships makes it possible to speak of God without the world and thus distinguish the Creator from a demiurge. By way of this contrast the freedom of God to create can be conceived as a freedom that has no presuppositions apart from God's own being and is in this way truly infinite freedom.

2. Understanding the Creator as the triune God helps to specify the relationship between God and the world by conceiving the triune being of God as the ground of creation. While emphasising the freedom of God to create, the Christian understanding of creation has also insisted that creation is not

[10] A classical expression of this view can be found in Irenaeus, *Adv. haer.* II, 1, 1 and II, 10, 4. Cf. on these passages Gerhard May, *Schöpfung aus dem Nichts. Die Entstehung der Lehre von der creatio ex nihilo* (Berlin and New York: de Gruyter, 1978), pp. 167ff.

[11] A typical example is Athanasius' rejoinder to the Arian objection that if the Son who is the offspring of the Father is eternal, then the world which the Father has made must also be considered eternal. Athanasius argues that that which is made is external to the maker, but the Son is 'the own offspring of his (i.e. the Father's) *ousia*' (*Or. con. Ar.* I, 29); cf. the exposition of the relationship of Father and Son as an internal relation in I, 14. Cf. on the interpretation of the passage, Torrance, *Trinitarian Faith*, pp. 86f. and Hanson, *Search*, p. 430.

[12] The application of the *homoousios*-formula in clarifying God's relationship to creation by contrasting it with the relationship of the Father and the Son is part of what Torrance has called the 'hermeneutical significance of the *homoousion*', cf. *Trinitarian Faith*, pp. 125ff.

the result of an arbitrary act of the divine will. God continually preserves and sustains creation so that it has its own divinely-given created, that is, finite permanence.[13] Creation has therefore also to be understood as an expression of the love of God who remains faithful to what he has created in love. If love comes to expression in God's granting finite permanence to a freely created world, it cannot be a temporary attitude adopted by God's will but has to be a relationship that is anchored in God's being.

Here we come to the point where the doctrine of the Trinity not only plays a critical role for the doctrine of creation in securing the distinction between Creator and creation, but also plays a constructive role in specifying the kind of relationship that exists between Creator and creation. The doctrine of the Trinity is the form in which freedom and love are thought together in the Christian understanding of God. The God who is the one who loves in freedom – 'der Liebende in der Freiheit' to quote Karl Barth[14] – is the trinitarian God. The Son is eternally the object of the love of the Father without being the necessary outflow of the Father's being, and therefore the Son can respond to the love of the Father by doing his will in the Spirit who is freedom. Freedom and love which characterise the relationship of God to what he is not are in this way rooted in who God is as Father, Son and Spirit. In the triune God freedom and love mediate difference in the personal particularity of otherness and unity in communion. And they do so in a way that is ontologically constitutive for the being of the trinitarian persons. When this God creates, it is a creativity of freedom and love.

If the being of God the Creator is understood in a consistently trinitarian sense, difference and communion are not only categories which characterise the relationship of God to that which is not God, but they are rooted in the triune divine being. The person of the Son is the principle of otherness, of difference in the Trinity, eternally generated by the unoriginated Father, the eternal principle of all origin, as the personal other of his love. Because of his origin in the freedom of the Father, the Son can freely respond to the Father by doing his

---

[13] Cf. Calvin's statement: 'It were cold and lifeless to represent God as a momentary Creator, who completed his work once and for all, and then left it. Here, especially, we must dissent from the profane, and maintain that the presence of the divine power is conspicuous, not less in the perpetual condition of the world than in its first creation.' *Institutes of the Christian Religion*, translated by Henry Beveridge (Grand Rapids, Mich.: Wm. B. Eerdmans, repr. 1995), I, 16.1, p. 171.

[14] Cf. *Die Kirchliche Dogmatik* 2/1 § 28, p. 288.

will, by making the will of the Father his own. Without the difference of the Son from the Father there can be no personal unity as communion in their relationship. The person of the Spirit is the principle of communion in the Trinity through whom the Father and the Son give and receive the communion of their freedom. God is not only free in relation to what God is not, but he is free in the personal communion that God is. God loves not only that which is the created object of his love, but God *is* love in the relationship that is God's being.[15]

This has important implications. God does not *become* active when he acts as the Creator, he *is* active in the immanent actions which constitute the triune divine life and thus are the ground of the possibility of God's *opera ad extra*.[16] God does not become relational with the creation of the world, rather his relational being is the ground and end of his relation to what he is not. We can summarise that in the following way: The ground of creation is the triune love of God. Since the triune being of God is the communion constituted in the freedom of

---

[15] Wolfhart Pannenberg has given a most illuminating account of the 'trinitarian origin of the act of creation' in his *Systematische Theologie* Bd. II (Göttingen: Vandenhoeck & Ruprecht, 1991), pp. 34–49. He takes up Hegel's interpretation of the Son as the principle of difference, but criticises him for understanding the Son merely as the *logical* instance of difference and not *personally* as the free principle of his self-differentiation from the Father, cf. *Systematische Theologie* II, p. 46. While Pannenberg is correct in criticising the development of the view of the Son as the principle of otherness in Hegel's 'philosophical monism' (p. 46), there remain some doubts whether his own account does not emphasise the *self*-distinction of the Son from the Father to such an extent that the Spirit who is the personal principle of communion in the Trinity and of the communion of creation with God is to some extent marginalised. Would it not be more appropriate to see the Son distinguishing himself from the Father in the Spirit by relating to the Father through the Spirit? In this way difference and communion would be mediated through the Son and the Spirit and not through an act of *self*-distinction which seems to abstract from the relationships which constitute the trinitarian persons in communion. If the personal particularity and the communion of the trinitarian persons are constituted through their relations with one another, the *self*-differentiation of one person from another would seem to be an incomplete, and therefore possibly misleading, description of the trinitarian relations. However, this seems more a matter of emphasis than of substance.

[16] Pannenberg (*Systematische Theologie* II, p. 18) has emphasised that the characterisation of the immanent relations of the Trinity as actions in Western trinitarian theology is an important improvement on the Eastern, more specifically Palamite notion of the divine energies which are uncreated, but must nevertheless be distinguished from the divine essence. If the *actiones immanentes* are seen as corollaries of the immanent relations in the Trinity and so as the ground of the *actiones transeuntes* in the relations of the Trinity *ad extra*, God's trinitarian being can in itself be conceived as active. Pannenberg sees the beginning of this development in the general application of the concept of *processio* which is not restricted to the procession of the Spirit in Richard of St. Victor's doctrine of the Trinity.

the relationship of the persons of Father, Son and Spirit, creation can be an act of freedom that is not an arbitrary exercise of the divine will but an expression of the being of God as love.

One point, however, must be added immediately. The understanding of God's love as trinitarian love is a necessary correlate of seeing the love of God as the ground of creation. The love of God can only be a freely creative love if it does not fall under the category of 'need-love', that is, if it is not the expression of a deficiency in God's being which could only be overcome in a relationship of love.[17] This is traditionally expressed by emphasising the perfection of God the Creator: God does not create in order to compensate for an inherent imperfection of the divine being. Understanding perfection as the perfection of the triune God adds an important element here. The communion of the persons of Father, Son and Spirit is a perfect communion, it is not in need of co-opting further members in order to find fulfilment. The creative love of the triune God is the free communication of his love to an object of the divine love which God freely posits as an expression of the perfection of the divine life and not as a compensation for its imperfection. Understanding creation as an act grounded in the perfect being of the triune God implies understanding creation as a completely gratuitous gift.

3. A trinitarian understanding of God the Creator integrates creation into the overall framework of divine action and this leads to a view of creation as a complex, that is trinitarianly differentiated, act. The trinitarian understanding of creation came into being precisely through this sort of integration. It is faith's insight that salvation in Christ is ultimate that leads to the recognition that the one 'through whom our release is secured and our sins are forgiven' does not only enter the stage of the drama of creation in the third act, but constitutes its beginning: 'In him everything in heaven and on earth was created' (Colossians 1.15, 16). Because he is the mediator of creation in the first place 'all things are held together in him' and therefore 'the universe, everything in heaven and on earth, might be brought into a unity in Christ' (Colossians 1.17 and Ephesians 1.10). The recognition of the eschatological ultimacy of salvation leads to an understanding of creation as mediated by, integrated in and ordered towards Christ. In the same way

[17] Cf. on the notion of 'need-love' the analysis by Vincent Brümmer in his *The Model of Love. A Study in Philosophical Theology* (Cambridge: Cambridge University Press, 1993), pp. 109–27. Brümmer, however, draws different systematic conclusions.

the Spirit as 'the firstfruits of the harvest to come' (Romans 8.23), the anticipatory presence of eschatological consummation, comes to be interpreted as the life-giver who from the beginning energises creation to enable it to respond to its Creator. The first steps taken on the road towards an understanding of the triune being of the Creator are the result of grasping the unity of divine action in creation, reconciliation and eschatological perfection as an implication of the ultimacy of salvation. Therefore the unity of God finally came to be conceived as the triunity of divine being mediated in the communion of Father, Son and Spirit. Speaking of God the triune Creator enables us to integrate creation into the overall pattern of divine action that is indicated by a trinitarian understanding of God. It is in this way made possible to express the purpose of creation by pointing to the unity of divine action implied in the trinitarian understanding of God: God creates in order to bring to perfection community with his reconciled creation. Luther expresses this almost tersely in the Greater Catechism: 'For He created us in order that He might redeem and sanctify us.'[18] God's creative love is placed into the context of God's saving and perfecting love and vice versa.

Conceiving the Creator as the triune God has another important corollary. Not only is creation related to reconciliation and perfection, it also appears as a complex act, an internally differentiated activity to which Father, Son and Spirit contribute specific aspects reflecting the particularity of their personal being in the unity of their action. One of the attempts to spell out this internal, that is trinitarian, differentiation of the unity of divine action, is that of Calvin: 'This distinction is, that to the Father is attributed the beginning of action, the fountain and source of all things; to the Son wisdom, counsel, and arrangement in action, while the energy and efficacy of action is assigned to the Spirit.'[19] An understanding of creation which is based on the notion of the triune Creator cannot be reduced to addressing the question 'Why is there something and not nothing?', because it is not only concerned with the question of the ground of being. Discourse about

---

[18] *Luther's Primary Works together with his Shorter and Larger Catechisms.* Translated into English, edited with theological and historical essays by H. Wace and C. A. Buchheim (London, 1896), p. 106. Cf. my paper 'The Triune God of Grace. The Doctrine of the Trinity in the Theology of the Reformers', in James M. Byrne (ed.), *The Christian Understanding of God Today. Theological Colloquium on the Occasion of the 400th Anniversary of the Foundation of Trinity College, Dublin* (Dublin: The Columba Press, 1993), pp. 49–64.

[19] *Institutes of the Christian Religion*, translated by Henry Beveridge, I, 13, 18, p. 126.

creation as the work of the triune Creator also encompasses talking of God as the source of the intelligibility of creation and as the giver of its life, its capacity to respond to God in its created processes of self-transcendence and self-integration.

These three points illustrate the methodological point about the interrelated character of doctrinal formulations in Christian dogmatics I mentioned at the beginning of this section. Dogmatic statements about the triune Creator cannot simply be inferred from observation of the natural order in the way a natural theology would have to attempt to do it, nor can they be developed merely on the basis of general revelation. They are based on the tradition of faith of the Christian community by interpreting this tradition as the historical, and that implies dynamic, changing and fallible, human response to God's self-disclosure in Jesus Christ as the self-identification of God in the mutual identification of Father, Son and Spirit. Although the view of God as the triune Creator is not based on the observation of the created order nor inferred from supposedly general revelation, it nevertheless implies a specific understanding of creation.

III   Creation: *creatio* and *creatura*

The word 'creation' has a twofold sense which points to a theologically significant distinction and relationship. On the one hand it can denote the act of creating, on the other hand it can refer to the result of such creating. The Latin terminology of theology can distinguish the two senses by using different terms: *creatio* for the act of creating, *creatura* for the result of such creating. A theology of creation can be developed from two complementary perspectives. Every theological account of creation as *creatio*, as divine creating, implies an account of creation as *creatura*, an account of createdness as the fundamental characteristic of the world; every theological description of the world as *creatura* presupposes a view of its constitution, an account of divine creating. Both are strictly complementary and only together can they provide the outlines of a theology of creation. In the following sections I shall try to summarise such basic outlines by referring to three classical formulae of the Christian doctrine of creation.

1. *Absolute giving: creatio ex nihilo*

The thesis that divine creating is *creatio ex nihilo*, creation from nothing, developed in the first centuries of Christian doctrine as the summary of the core elements of the biblical witness to creation over against rival religious and philo-

sophical views.[20] It is more a signpost to reflection than a clear
and distinct result of such a reflection, and the debate over its
interpretation has continued until this day.[21] Yet it is anything
but an instance of the dubious *credo quia absurdum*. The
expression is clear in what it rejects. Its target is the assumption that God's creativity is in some sense dependent on some
already existing material, perhaps *materia informis*, unformed
matter. What is rejected is the image of creating which interprets it according to the pattern of the demiurge in Plato's
Timaeus as the shaping of given matter.[22] The offence of this
notion of creating lies in its dualistic implications which seem
to suggest that there are somehow two creative principles,
one actively and one passively creative, God and matter. In
this sense Theophilus of Antioch emphasised that God's
creativity has, unlike the creativity of the human artist, no
presupposition, and Irenaeus stressed that matter is not a
presupposition but a result of God's free creativity.[23] In
rejecting views of creating as shaping, the patristic writers who
established the formula could take up and develop the biblical
teaching of the sovereign freedom of God the Creator. Their
critical achievement is to distinguish the notions of freedom
and shaping. If God's creative freedom is truly infinite,
unbounded by anything external to God, it cannot be interpreted as the shaping of something given. The world is 'created,
but not from something' as Anselm paraphrased the formula
in his discussion in chapters 8 and 11 of his *Monologion*.[24]

---

[20] Cf. the exhaustive account by Gerhard May in his book *Schöpfung aus dem Nichts*, above n. 12.

[21] For a sophisticated contemporary interpretation cf. Eberhard Wölfel, *Welt als Schöpfung. Zu den Fundamentalsätzen der christlichen Schöpfungslehre heute* (München: Christian Kaiser, 1981).

[22] *Timaeus* 28A – 38A. The leading metaphor in the mythological account is the imposition of order on an existing state of disorder.

[23] Theophilus of Antioch, *Ad Aut*. I, 4 and 8; II, 4. Irenaeus, *Adv. haer*. II, 10, 4.

[24] Anselm offers in chapter 8 a sophisticated semantic analysis of the expression '*ex nihilo*'. He distinguishes three senses in which the expression can be
understood: the first is meaningless, the second evidently false, and only the
third points the way to a theologically appropriate understanding. In the
first sense the expression could be understood to convey that nothing was
made, if we say that something was made from nothing. It is like asking
about a silent person 'what is she talking about?' and receiving the answer
'nothing', meaning 'she is not talking at all'. In this sense '*ex nihilo*' means
'*necquaquam factum est*' and to say this of created beings is meaningless.
The second sense can be meaningfully stated, but what is stated cannot be
true. In this second sense 'nothing' is interpreted as some sort of 'something'
from which something was made (*quasi ipsum nihil sit aliquid existens, ex
quo possit aliquid fieri*). The third sense is the interpretation of the phrase
where we recognise that something was made, but that there is no
'something' from which it was made (*esse quidem factum, sed non esse*

What the formula states positively can perhaps be paraphrased in the following way. There is no given for God's
creativity, because it has the character of absolute giving. God's
creativity does not presuppose anything antecendently given,
apart from God's own triune being as the ground for creation.
All other giving is, compared with God's creative giving, only
relative since it presupposes antecedent conditions for the
act of giving, the existence of something to give, for instance.
God's creative giving is absolute in having no antecedent
conditions apart from God's own triune being of love. It is
absolute insofar as God's creative giving is the giving of being
to something that is not before the Creator gives it. 'Absolute
giving' as the expression paraphrasing the positive content of
the *creatio ex nihilo* formula interprets the relationship of God
to all that is not God as an active productive relationship in
which everything that is has its being in its relationship to
God the Creator. Through the absolute giving of creation God
is the ground of the possibility of all worldly being.

Interpreted in this radical sense, creation as absolute giving
excludes an understanding of creation that reduces it to the
actualisation of individual essences already existing as ideas
in the divine mind. If creating is only the actualisation of
already existing possible beings – as has recently been emphasised both by Wolfhart Pannenberg and David Burrell[25] –
creatio ex nihilo is again rendered as something inferior to
absolute giving, since the possible individuals already are what
they are before they are actualised. Creation can only be

---

aliquid, unde sit factum). Anselm builds his further reflections on this
interpretation of the phrase. Cf. Anselm von Canterbury, *Monologion*.
Lateinisch-deutsche Ausgabe von Franciscus Salesius Schmitt O.S.B.
(Frankfurt: Fromman (Holzboog), 1964), pp. 62–6.

[25] In his discussion of the question whether in creating God's will depends on
prior ideas in the divine mind, a view that was denied by Descartes but
affirmed by Leibniz, Pannenberg concludes that a contemporary theology of
creation should refrain from employing this notion. In his view it suggests
an anthropomorphic conception of the relationship of the divine mind and
the divine will and reduces the emphasis on the contingence and historical
character of created reality which is central to the biblical understanding of
creation. Cf. *Systematische Theologie* II, pp. 41f. With regard to Linda
Zagzebski's account of creation in her paper 'Individual Essence and the
Creation', in Thomas Morris (ed.), *Divine and Human Action* (Ithaca, N.Y.:
Cornell University Press, 1988), pp. 119–43, David Burrell raises (and
answers) the following question: 'Can one speak of individuals *before* they
exist; is it coherent to speak in this sense of "individual essences"? Again,
one need not picture them over against the creator; in fact, one may consider
them to be "in the mind of God", thereby preserving, it seems, the primacy of
the One from whom everything comes. Yet the questionable metaphysical

absolute giving if what things are and that they are, the
possible and the actual, have their source in God's freedom
to give, that is, to give being to what is not God. Only in
this sense can creation be conceived as absolute giving, as
gratuitous origination.

2. *The absolute gift: the contingent creature*

The understanding of the act of creating as *creatio ex nihilo*
implies a view of the world as creation, as *creatura*, as an
absolute gift. The contingent status of the being of the world is
the strict correlate of the freedom of the Creator exercised as
absolute giving. The world exists as creation, as *creatura*, as
contingent being; its possibility of existence, its particular
constitution and its structures are rooted in its permanent
ontological dependence on God the Creator. This contingence
of the world as creation not only characterises its being, its
ontological status, but also its intelligibility and its created
goodness. As an absolute gift the being of the world is
contingent being in that it does not have to be but could not be.
It has neither control over its origin nor over its end. However,
it makes all the difference to our understanding of the world if
this contingent character of the being and constitution of the
world is regarded as *a given* that is to be explored and
explained or as *a gift* that is to be responded to. Seeing, as
Christian dogmatics does, the world as an absolute gift,
strictly correlated to the notion of God's absolute giving,
releases and requires quite a different set of attitudes to
everything that is created. A given may provoke wonder and
puzzlement, it requires exploration and explanation. Ultimately, its 'givenness' is a challenge to deal with it as far as we
can and to adopt a fatalistic attitude to those aspects we cannot
deal with: the characteristic marks of a 'naturalistic' understanding of the world. Seeing creation, including ourselves, as
a gift means that in relating to the gift we are relating to the
giver. Interpreted as a gift, the meaning of the contingent being
of creation, including its origin and its end, depends on the
giver of this gift.

---

point does not lie in the picturing, but in the assertion that "they" are
before their coming into existence. And since "coming-into-existence" does
not represent a change in *them,* any more than the act of creating involves
motion, we quickly realise that any talk of "individual essences", or
"exemplars" of individuals in the mind of God, makes the act of creating
into that of a demiurge.' David B. Burrell, C.S.C., *Freedom and Creation in
Three Traditions* (Notre Dame, Indiana: University of Notre Dame Press,
1993).

3. Faithful giving: creatio continuata

The formula of continued creation, *creatio continuata,* presupposes the doctrine of gratuitous origination. However, it develops it in such a way as to bring out its anti-deistic implications. Creation is not restricted to a single event 'in the beginning'; it accompanies the history of creation and maintains the contingent being of the world in time. Creation as *creatura* is not left to its own devices, a clockwork that functions mechanically once it has been set in motion. Rather, the notion of continued creation expands the meaning of creation in such a way that God's creative relationship to creation is depicted as present to creation at every moment of its life. The God Christians confess as the Creator is not the divine clockmaker who takes early retirement once his work is completed. The God of continued creation maintains the creation in its created structures and dynamic through time and so conserves its being. Both elements of the formula are important. Creation is *continued,* the world is upheld in the structures given to it from the beginning, it cannot grow out of its dependence on the Creator. Without God granting it being at every moment it would vanish into nothingness. Nevertheless, God's continued creation is still creation, it is still the giving of novelty that was not before in the process of the world. Both aspects, continuity of creation and creation as the bringing about of novelty – Luther's famous *'creare est semper novum facere'*[26] – illuminate the character of the world we live in, with its interplay between rule-governed structures and free spontaneity.

The doctrine of *creatio continuata* is an expression of God's creative faithful giving. This receives strong support from the view that God's freedom to create is grounded in the triune divine being. Remaining faithful in creating is an expression of the constancy of God's being which is reflected in God's remaining faithful to creation. However, God's faithfulness in

---

[26] This phrase which combines the emphasis on continuity (*semper*) and on novelty (*novum*) is from the *Resolutiones disputationum de indulgentiarum virtute* 1518. The full quotation explains its relationship to *conservatio* and *creatio continuata*: 'Impossibile est ulla perseverantia creatura, nisi assidue accipiat magis ac magis; inde enim dicunt acuti quidam, quod conservatio rei sit eius continuata creatio. Sed creare est semper novum facere, ut etiam patet in rivulis, radiis, calore, frigore, maxime dum sunt extra suum principium. Quare et spirituali calori id est amori dei, in animabus opus est continuata conservatio (donec absorbeantur in suum principium divinum) ac per hoc et augmentum, etiam si verum esset, quod essent perfectae, licet extra deum esse nec pervenisse et esse perfectum sint contraria.' WA 1, 563, 6–13. Cf. David Löfgren, *Die Theologie der Schöpfung bei Luther* (Göttingen: Vandenhoeck & Ruprecht, 1960).

creative giving goes beyond the mere conservation of creation. Following the Lutheran and Reformed divines of the seventeenth century one can attempt to specify particular aspects of continued creation as an expression of God's faithful giving.[27] Continued creation includes the *concursus divinus*, the way in which God's creative activity is a necessary condition for all activity in creation so that all that occurs falls within the governing, the *gubernatio* of divine providence. Permitting evil and sin (*permissio*) as an expression of the relative autonomy of creation over against the Creator – an autonomy that can be as radical as the open contradiction against the Creator – while at the same time impeding the consequences of sin and evil (*impeditio*) so that they do not lead to the ultimate self-destruction of the creature, can in this way be interpreted as aspects of the faithfulness of God's giving. However, the theologians of the seventeenth century were never in any doubt that the ultimate goal-directedness (*directio*) remains God's privilege. It is an expression of the faithfulness of the Creator

---

[27] The development of the doctrine of *creatio continuata* beyond the notion of a conservation of creation so that it can be treated from the perspective of the *gubernatio* in the framework of the doctrine of providence is demonstrated by the form it receives in the textbook on Christian doctrine by J. Fr. König which Carl Heinz Ratschow uses as the paradigmatic example for the teaching of the so-called Lutheran orthodoxy of the seventeenth century in his *Lutherische Dogmatik zwischen Reformation und Aufklärung*, part II (Gütersloh: Gütersloher Verlagshaus, 1966). The interesting aspect for our theme consists in the fact that these conceptualisations of the ways in which God is creatively present to creation all have significant ethical implications insofar as they give indirect descriptions of the possibilities of human action by specifying the ways in which human agency is enabled and restricted by God's continued creating. This can be illustrated from König's definitions of the concepts which Ratschow cites (pp. 209ff.):

– Concursus est actus providentiae divinae, quo deus influxu generali in actiones et effectus causae secundae, qua tales, se ipso immediate et simul cum ea et iuxta exigentiam uniuscuiusque suaviter influit.
– Gubernatio est actus providentiae divinae, quo deus creaturas in viribus, actionibus et passionibus suis decenter ordinat, ad creatoris gloriam et universi huius bonum, ac piorum imprimis salutem.
– Permissio est actus providentiae gubernatricis, quo deus creaturas rationales ad peccandum sua sponte sese inclinantes, per impeditimenta, quibus agens finitum resistere nequit vel quibus non resiturum novit, a malo lege vetito non retrahit, sed iustis de causis in peccata ruere sinit.
– Impeditio est actus providentiae gubernatricis, quo deus actionum creaturarum pro arbitrio suo constringit, ne effectum dent, quod vel naturali, vel libera agendi vi alias efficerent.
– Directio est actus providentiae gubernatricis, quo deus creaturarum actiones ita moderatur, ut ferantur in obiectum ab infinito agente intentum et in finem ab eodem praestitutum
– Determinatio est actus providentiae gubernatricis, quo deus creaturarum viribus, actionibus et passionibus certos terminos, intra quos se contineant, tum ratione temporis, tum ratione magnitudinis et gradus, constituit.

to the purpose of creation. In this way God enables and restricts the relative autonomy of created agencies by determining the boundaries of their activity (*determinatio*). Not the least important, but often neglected aspect of the doctrine of continued creation is that the faithfulness of God's giving remains an element of God's actions in reconciling and perfecting creation. Salvation is therefore not salvation *from* the world, but salvation *of* the world as creation. It is an expression of God's faithful giving and not its renunciation, as gnostics of all ages would want us to believe.

4. The gift maintained: scope for responsibilty

One crucial aspect of the doctrine of *creatio continuata*, paraphrased as the faithfulness of God's giving, is the understanding of the structure of the world as creation it has as its correlate. While the doctrine of *creatio ex nihilo* indicates the constitutive ontological dependence of the contingent being of creation on God's creativity as absolute giving, the doctrine of continued divine creating points to the finite permanence and reliability of the structures of creation maintained in God's faithful giving. Continued divine creating is the condition for the possibility of the relative autonomy of the natural processes of the world and of created freedom in it. The relative constancy of the order of creation is the gift maintained in God's faithfulness. Characterising this constancy as relative is to be understood in the strict sense of being relative to God's continuous creating. This comprises both elements of rule-directed structures and of spontaneity, making possible the interplay between structure and spontaneity which characterises the created order.[28] This is a contingent but not a deterministic order so that it provides the scope for human action in finite created freedom and finite responsibility.

It is the distinction of the human creature, created in the image of God, to be called to exercise its created destiny in finite freedom. Finite, created freedom is the freedom which is a gift of God the Creator, freedom which is passively constituted for the human agent and dependent for its exercise on this passive constitution.[29] Where it interprets itself as

[28] Ample illustrations can be found in Ilya Prigogine and Isabelle Stengers, *Order Out of Chaos. Man's New Dialogue with Nature* (London: Fontana, 1985). For an illuminating discussion of the implications of this view, cf. the chapter 'Relation and Relativity. The Trinity and the Created World', in Colin E. Gunton, *The Promise of Trinitarian Theology* (Edinburgh: T. & T. Clark, 2nd edition, 1997), pp. 137–57.

[29] Cf. my article 'Imago Libertatis: Human and Divine Freedom', in Colin E. Gunton (ed.), *God and Freedom. Essays in Historical and Systematic Theology* (Edinburgh: T. & T. Clark, 1995), pp. 57–81.

absolute self-created freedom and denies its character as a gift, it falls into bondage from which it can find no escape. Finite freedom is the created other of God's being as triune love called to respond to this love in living in fellowship with God by doing God's will. The exercise of finite freedom depends on the gift maintained, on the faithfulness of the Creator sustaining the structures of creation. Freedom can only be exercised where scope is given for intentional action understood as the carrying out of a consciously chosen intention. Only where the connection between intention and effective action can be secured is it possible to assume and to ascribe responsibility. The responsibility of human freedom therefore rests on the faithfulness of the Creator in maintaining a relatively stable environment for action so that we are able to discern the effects, possible and actual, which are produced in actualising our intentions. The relative constancy of the contingent order of creation, the gift maintained in the faithful giving of the Creator, is in this way understood as the ground of the possibility of human freedom and responsibility. The radical nature of this faithfulness becomes clear when we see it, as we have just mentioned, as an essential element in God's reconciling and perfecting action. Here the full depth of God's faithful giving is revealed as it is maintained against the human contradiction against God, the abuse of created freedom and an escape into unaccountability. Reconciliation as the recreation of finite freedom that had been lost, and perfection as the transformation of that which had been perverted, disclose the radical nature of God's faithfulness.

5. *The end of giving: finis creationis est gloria Dei*

The third central statement of the understanding of creation is one which is most often overlooked, although it is widely documented in the theological tradition from Thomas Aquinas to the Lutheran and Reformed divines of the seventeenth century. Creation as *creatura* is not the end, the objective, the ultimate goal of creation as God's *creatio*. The end of God's creating is God's own glory.[30] One can well understand why this statement is treated with such scepticism. It seems to reflect an attitude which in human terms would reflect the

---

[30] Cf. the sources cited in C. H. Ratschow, *Lutherische Dogmatik*, pp. 163 and 167. This notion provides the thrust of Friedrich Wilhelm Graf's perceptive criticism of some tendencies of modern ethics of creation in his article 'Von der creatio ex nihilo zur "Bewahrung der Schöpfung". Dogmatische Erwägungen zur Frage nach einer möglichen ethischen Relevanz der Schöpfungslehre', *Zeitschrift für Theologie und Kirche* 87 (1990), pp. 206–23.

climax of the psychopathology of sin: *amor sui*, self-love. On the basis of a unipersonalist understanding of God the statement would indeed come close to a theological catastrophe. It is here that the understanding of God as the triune Creator introduces quite a different perspective. If God is the communion of the persons of Father, Son and Spirit and if the freedom in love of the divine triunity is the ground of creation; further, if the faithfulness of God is the faithfulness rooted in the divine being, it does not seem contradictory to see the end of creation in God's triune being. However, on the basis of a trinitarian understanding of God, glory is not a self-directed attitude, but the mutuality of glorifying the other and receiving glory from the other which constitutes the communion of the divine life. Trinitarian glory is communicating glory and communicated glory. Just as the mediation of difference as otherness and unity as communion is the ground of creating in love and freedom so it is the end of creating in giving and receiving glory. The pattern of mutual glory is the pattern of the triune divine life: 'Father, the hour has come. Glorify your Son, that the Son may glorify you' (John 17.1). Including creation into the mutuality of communicating and communicated glory is the end of God's creating, which in this way defines the destiny of creation to join with the Spirit in the glorification of the Father through the Son.

6. The destiny of creation: the glory of the giver

The immediate implication of seeing the glory of God as the end of creation is an explicit restriction of human interaction with the world of creation. For the dogmatics of the seventeenth century the glory of God as the objective of creation had a regulative function for the human relationship to the world: its use for the human is at best an intermediate end of creation, it is never its ultimate end.[31] Perhaps the ecological crisis has heightened our awareness of an understanding of the end of creation where one interpretation is definitely excluded: that it may be seen as directed to the greater glory of the human. This is already one important implication of the dogmatic account of creation for an ethic of createdness: If the self-glorification of the human creature is excluded by seeing the glory of God as the end of creation, the utility of creation for humans may never become the ultimate objective of human interaction with creation. The theocentric view of the end of creation prevents the kind of anthropocentric attitude where the greater glory of

---

[31] Consequently *gloria dei* as the *finis ultimus* of creation is distinguished from *utilitas hominum* as the *finis intermedius creationis*.

the human has to be achieved at the expense of the rest of creation.

Has the thesis that the end of creation is the glory of the giver perhaps other, more constructive implications, going beyond the regulative function we have just described? If glory as the end of creation follows the pattern of trinitarian love, finding self-fulfilment in affirming the being of the other and being affirmed by the freely given affirmation of one's own being by the other, it points to a pattern of relationships that transcends the self-directed attempt at self-affirmation which lies at the root of many self-destructive tendencies in creation. 'To the glory of God' then defines a direction of human action that is the opposite of pride as the attempt at seeking self-fulfilment at the expense of the other.

IV The Christian Community: The Social Shape of an Ethic of Createdness

The Christian community, the church, does not enter reflections on the theology of creation as an after-thought. It is an inherent presupposition of dogmatic reflection on creation, and not only for methodological reasons. It is the being of the church which requires the integration of the church into the presuppositions of dogmatic reflection on creation. The recent statement by the Leuenberg Fellowship of Churches, adopted at its General Assembly at Vienna in May 1994 with the title 'The Church of Jesus Christ', summarises the teaching of the Reformation on the being of the church in the following way: 'The church has its foundation in the Word of the triune God. It is the creature of the Word calling for faith by which God reconciles and relates the alienated and rebellious human race to himself by justifying and sanctifying it in Christ, by renewing it in the Holy Spirit and by calling it to be his people.'[32] If the being of the church has its origin in the Word of the triune God, and if its ontological status is that of the creature of Word, the Christian community has the same ontological constitution as creation as a whole.[33] It has been

[32] Leuenberg Fellowship of Churches, *The Church of Jesus Christ. The Contribution of the Reformation towards Ecumenical Dialogue on Church Unity* (Frankfurt: Otto Lembeck, 1995), p. 88.
[33] Cf. my paper 'The Creature of the Word: Recovering the Ecclesiology of the Reformers', in *On Being the Church. Essays on the Christian Community*, edited by Colin E. Gunton and Daniel W. Hardy (Edinburgh: T. & T. Clark 1989), pp. 110–45. On the character of the church as communion, cf. my paper: 'Kirche als Communio', in *Marburger Jahrbuch Theologie, vol. VIII: Kirche*, edited by Wilfried Härle and Reiner Preul (Marburg, 1996), pp. 11–46.

one of the difficulties of ecclesiological thought in the West that this identity of ontological constitution has been obscured by appropriating creation exclusively to the Father and the institution of the church exclusively to the Son, so that creation and redemption appeared to be discontinuous in a sense that has blurred important aspects of the understanding of both creation *and* redemption. The upshot of this was a separation of created sociality and redeemed sociality which – as Daniel Hardy has shown[34] – runs the risk of rendering both implausible. The theological task consists in showing that a trinitarian understanding of God and, consequently, the trinitarian understanding of the agency of God, can overcome the one-sidedness of a patromonistic understanding of creation and of a Christomonistic understanding of the church.

The church owes its being along with the whole of creation to the absolute giving of the triune God which is grounded in the love-mediating otherness and communion that is the being of this God. The fact that the constitution of the church happens as the justification of the sinner in Christ enhances the similarity between the creation of the world and the creation of the church. Just as the absolute giving of the Creator is not dependent on an already existing matter and is therefore an act of sovereign freedom, so the justification of the sinner is not dependent on any meritorious act on the part of the sinner, but on the imputation of the alien righteousness of Christ to the sinner. Being made righteous is, just like being created, an absolute gift. The same parallel is there concerning the being of creation and the church in time: they are being preserved by God's faithful giving in spite of their contradiction against God or their failure to respond appropriately to the source of their being. God's maintaining the conditions for its existence defines for the church the scope of its responsibility just as it does for all human creatures. And just as creation has its end not in itself, so the church has its end in the Kingdom of God, the celebration of the glory of the giver in the New Jerusalem, which is brought about – according to the promise of the gospel – by God's sovereign freedom and not by the causality of created, not even ecclesial, agencies.

However, pointing out this parallelism of ontological constitution between creation and the church does not yet do enough to grasp their relation. Is the world the church? Or are they two separate realities? What is their relationship? Perhaps the relationship can be described in the following way:

[34] Cf. his essay 'Created and Redeemed Sociality', in *On Being the Church*, pp. 21–47.

Because the church experiences in its own being that it has the source of its existence in the absolute giving of God, that it owes its preservation in time to the faithfulness of God's giving, and that it has its destiny in giving glory to the giver, it can recognise divine giving as the source of the existence, the continuity and the destiny of all created being. At the same time the church can recognise its own being as part of the process in which God actualises the purpose of creation: 'For He created us in order that He might redeem and sanctify us.' The particular being of the church is its universal significance. In the being of the church creation becomes aware of its constitution and purpose. Therefore it is the particular distinction of the church that, in virtue of its own constitution, it can apprehend and acknowledge createdness as the fundamental feature of all reality. This acknowledgement finds expression in two forms: as Christian faith and as Christian life. Christian faith as fundamental trust in God, Father, Son and Spirit, is the acknowledgement that our existence, the meaning and norm of our being, and the final destiny of our life have their source and end in God who 'created us that He might redeem and sanctify us'. In Christian life this faith is appropriated as the fundamental orientation in all our actions, in our symbolising as well as in our organising activity. Both are fundamentally social in character. In spite of Kierkegaard it seems to me that the solitary Christian is a contradiction in terms. How then can createdness as the constitutive feature of the life of the Christian community, that through which it recognises the createdness of all being, function as the central term of an ethic, a policy of action in the Christian life?

Ethics can be described as being concerned with three broad areas of questions: questions about the possibilities of action, both objective and subjective, that is, concerning the presuppositions of action in a given field of action and concerning the capacities of agents to act; questions about the norms of action and the duties which follow from these norms; and questions about the Good, the values or ethical goods brought about by agents with certain capacities following certain norms of action in certain given circumstances. This corresponds roughly to the classical division between a theory of virtue, a theory of duties and a theory of the Good. Our thesis now is that in the ethics of the Christian community the notion of createdness as we have tried to develop it on the basis of dogmatic considerations should play a fundamental role in all three areas.

1. Human action that is attuned neither to the situation in which it occurs nor to the capacities of the agent is bound to

fail. At best it remains ineffective and at worst it becomes destructive for the circumstances of action or for the agents. A failure to adapt to the objective and subjective possibilities of action becomes disastrous not so much when it is a failure to adapt to variable features of the circumstances of action or the capacities of the agent as when it is failure to adapt to invariant features. Understanding the world and human agents in the world as created refers precisely to the invariant features of the possibilities of action. It demands that we see the fundamental features of the worldly circumstances in which we act and of our own capacities to act not as constituted by us, but as constituted for us. Seeing the world and ourselves as agents, as created, as the result of God's absolute giving, restricts our objective and subjective possibilities of action in such a way that it enables their success. The restriction that is demanded is precisely that we refrain from interpreting our relationship to the world in terms of absolute creativity. That has always been the promise of the serpent. The restriction of createdness as the enablement of action refers to all aspects of action from the choice of aims of action to the selection of means of action. The restriction placed upon our actions by the notion of createdness defines the possibilities for the exercise of finite freedom in a contingent world. The point of understanding both the world and ourselves as the result of God's absolute giving excludes the misunderstanding of seeing the non-human creation as God's gift to us which is then put at our disposal. Our capacities to act are just as much given to us as a gratuitous gift, not produced by us, as is the world in which we act. Humans act – that is the insight of the Christian community which understands itself as the creature of the divine Word – in the solidarity of all created being as God's absolute gift. It is therefore our responsibility to treat the world we act in as God's gift that is only entrusted to our responsible stewardship. And that entails that its character as a gift is to be respected in all our interaction with the non-human world so that it is not reduced to a mere given.

2. Human action can only avoid the charge of mere arbitrariness if it is directed by certain norms or rules of conduct. It is only morally qualifiable if these rules specify whether an action meets a given standard of goodness and therefore ought to be performed or whether it fails to meet this standard and therefore is to be refrained from. Norms of this kind function both in prescribing actions and in assessing their moral quality. For the Christian faith goodness is not an abstract and independent standard or value, but is primarily a divine

attribute which is communicated to creation in the sovereign
act of giving creation existence and order that is good.[35] The
created goodness of the created order becomes concrete in God's
maintaining the goodness of creation against the perversion of
goodness in the human contradiction against God. For the
Christian community which understands its own existence as
being preserved in time through God's faithfulness,
'createdness' indicates the horizon within which ethical norms
are formulated and human behaviour is assessed. Ethical
norms are therefore the *rules of response* to the faithful giving
of God the Creator and this defines the specific nature of
created responsibility. Christian ethics therefore understands
every act of relating to any part of the world as creation as
indirectly relating to God the Creator, thereby setting all
human action in the context of God's faithfulness to the
creation. The paradigm of such created responsibility is the
Ten Commandments in which relating to God, the first table
of the Commandments, forms the presupposition and the
standard of relating to creation, the second table of the
commandments. For an ethic of createdness in the Christian
community the universality of ethical norms is therefore not
grounded in one or several features of the world apart from its
relation to God, but precisely in this relation to God the Creator
which is the only universal relation that can be predicated of
all created being.

3. Human action has its distinguishing mark in being
intentional action, in being directed towards the actualisation
of consciously selected ends. It can only be ethical action if the
goal of action contributes to or supports the actualisation of
Good. For the Christian community which understands its own
being as being on the way towards the actualisation of the end
of creation, the glory of the Creator in the Kingdom of God, the
Kingdom of God is the Highest Good, the ultimate end of all
action. The crucial point for an ethic of createdness is, however,
that this final end of all action is not the product of created
action, but the objective of God's creating. For an ethic of
createdness the Highest Good lies outside the scope of human
action. The perfection of creation cannot be a human goal of
action, it is the prerogative of God whose absolute giving is the
origin of all creation. A Christian ethic of createdness receives
its particular character through the fact that all the aims and
ends of created action are orientated towards the Kingdom of
God as the Highest Good which will not be brought about by

[35] Cf. for this view the chapter 'God's Goodness and Human Morality' in my
book: *God: Action and Revelation* (Kampen: Kok Pharos, 1992), pp. 63–82.

any created agency. In this orientation of all ends of actions towards the Highest Good which it will not itself bring about lies the ground for the coherence of the policy of action of a Christian ethic of createdness. It can unify the manifold variety of aims and ends in focusing it on the Highest Good which is not an end of human action but the ultimate focus of all created action. A Christian ethic of createdness has its hallmark in the fact that the ground and end of human action is not its own product but that the absolute giving of God is the condition of the possibility of all created action and the glory of the Creator its ultimate fulfilment.

How can the form of action that is shaped by the ethic of createdness be exercised, how can it be reconstituted when we fail, how can it be developed and cultivated? How can Christian life gain constancy in growing and developing, provided it is, as Luther said, a permanent transition from vices to virtues? Ian Ramsay, who would normally not be suspected for replacing the rigours of thought with pious rhetoric, once remarked that 'a time of prayer can be like the Christian life in miniature'.[36] It seems indeed that prayer in its different forms of relating to God is the point in the Christian life where God's action and our action are grasped in their distinction and relationship and where the different aspects of createdness are expressed and enacted. In prayers of thanksgiving Christians acknowledge that their life and all there is owes its existence to God's absolute giving, and they recognise God's absolute gift in everything they experience and do. God's faithful giving is the focus of prayers of praise and of prayers of repentance expressing the trust that God will maintain the faithfulness of the Creator even where the human creatures have failed to respond appropriately to the gift of creation. Lamentation is an appeal to the faithfulness of God even where the will of the Creator is hidden in the world. Prayers of petition are in their most radical form prayers for the perfection of God's relationship with creation, prayers for the Kingdom to come so that the glory of the giver may be ultimately disclosed. The practice of prayer is fundamentally the relational enactment of the constitutive aspects of createdness, and so it shapes human action to find its origin, norms and ends in God's creative action. It is the point in the Christian life where the relationship between Christian faith and Christian life which is the foundation of the relationship between dogmatics and

[36] Ian T. Ramsey, *Our Understanding of Prayer* (London: SPCK, 1971), p. 22, quoted in Vincent Brümmer, *What Are We Doing When We Pray? A Philosophical Inquiry* (London: SCM Press, 1984), p. 112.

ethics is not only asserted but enacted. And it is in returning
to this focal point in its life that the Christian community can
discover and rediscover the sources of the ethic of createdness.

Index